1991

93

HEMMINGWAY, ERNEST 46610
H489ha Hardy, Richard E.
Hemingway, a psychological
portrait

**RENNER
LEARNING RESOURCES
CENTER
ELGIN COMMUNITY COLLEGE**
ELGIN, ILLINOIS

HEMINGWAY:
A Psychological Portrait

HEMINGWAY:
A Psychological Portrait

by Richard E. Hardy
and John G. Cull

BANNER BOOKS INTERNATIONAL

FIRST EDITION

Copyright © 1977 by Richard E. Hardy and John G. Cull. All rights reserved. No part of this publication may be reproduced, stored in a retrieval system, or transmitted, in any form or by any means, without prior written permission of the author and publisher. Manufactured in the United States of America.

ISBN 0-89491-007-8 Softcover
ISBN 0-89491-009-4 Hardcover

Library of Congress Catalog Card Number: 77-074327

BANNER BOOKS INTERNATIONAL
13415 Ventura Boulevard
Sherman Oaks, California 91423

To Judy, Carter, David and, of course, Jason,

and
Pat and Sallie Strong

and, in a totally different sense,
this book is further dedicated to the ambience of Key West. The white beaches, nestling between blue skies and bluer water, helped us discover some of the feelings Hemingway must have known. A special place, where he could blend love with adventure and grow in the ability to share.

ABOUT THE AUTHORS

Richard E. Hardy   John G. Cull

The authors have had an intense interest in the life and writings of Ernest Hemingway since their early high school days. They went to Key West and spent time there trying to experience what Hemingway saw, felt, and lived as a resident there during his most prolific writing periods. They bring to this revealing study the insights of modern clinical psychology together with the expertise of their years of experience in the field.

Richard E. Hardy is Professor and Chairman of the Department of Rehabilitation Counseling at Virginia Commonwealth University in Richmond, Virginia. A Diplomate in Counseling Psychology, American Board of Professional Psychology, Dr. Hardy received his Doctorate from the University of Maryland. He holds his B.S. from Virginia Polytechnic Institute & State University and his M.S. from Virginia Commonwealth University.

John G. Cull is Professor of Clinical Counseling Psychology at Our Lady of the Lake University, San Antonio, Texas. He obtained his Doctorate in Clinical/Counseling Psychology from Texas Tech University and his B.S. and M.S. degrees from Texas A&M University.

The authors have published and consulted extensively in the fields of psychology and rehabilitation. They have received both national and international awards for their work. *Hemingway: A Psychological Portrait* is their most recent collaborative project.

PREFACE

F. Scott Fitzgerald, an on-again, off-again friend of Ernest Hemingway, once said that biography is the falsest of arts. Certainly any attempt by biographers to create a hypothetical psychographic portrait of a person they never knew widens even further the range of difficulties associated with producing a valid biographical work.

We have maintained an intense personal interest in Ernest Hemingway since our high school days, having grown up with him through his gift of enlivening the literature of our land. Much of what we have to say in this book is speculative in nature and should be considered as historico-scientific conjecture. We feel that Hemingway himself, through his constant exploration of life and candid descriptions of his feelings and experiences, offered all readers the opportunity to know and understand one of the most fascinating persons of our time. The fact that we did not have the opportunity to know him personally was the motivating factor in the development of this book. We now feel we know him better, though only through our research of what he did, felt and wrote, and from what has been written and said about him by such perceptive contributors as Carlos Baker, William Barrett, Leicester Hemingway, Mary Hemingway, A. E. Hotchner, Constance Cappel Montgomery, William Seward and others.

We wish to acknowledge the very substantial contribution to this manuscript of Professor Leo A. Thralls and to thank him for his literary guidance and scholarship. We also extend appreciation to Terry Sherf for her skillful revision and editing.

As with any personality portrait, substantial biographical material must be woven into the fabric before hypotheses regarding the underlying personality can be put forth. We have presented substantial biographical material on Ernest Hemingway for just this purpose—to provide the framework on which we could build a montage of personality observations. Without a sound biographical foundation, based on careful research, the formulation of psychological considerations would be meaningless.

As you will note, our pace in recounting biographical material alters substantially in these pages. As we examine Hemingway's life, we isolate fewer and fewer specific incidents and turn instead to describing the high points of the years—finally phasing out even this descriptive approach. We have written in this manner because we feel the dynamics which provide the basic data on which the psychological portrait could be erected appear early in Hemingway's life. The biographical material on his later life is recounted primarily to provide continuity, and to dwell longer, with our readers, in the awesome presence which our study caused us to appreciate more than ever before.

Richard E. Hardy
John G. Cull

TABLE OF CONTENTS

Epilogue 9
Chapter **1** 10
Chapter **2** 16
Chapter **3** 19
Chapter **4** 25
Chapter **5** 36
Chapter **6** 39
Chapter **7** 50
Chapter **8** 60
Chapter **9** 63
Chapter **10** 66
Chapter **11** 69
Chapter **12** 72
Chapter **13** 75
Psychological
   Evaluation 81

EPILOGUE

On that morning, he awoke, dressed in his robe and slippers, and walked to the window. He gazed out silently across the beautiful Idaho countryside. The fields were green and etched with bright wildflowers, yet how dreary and bleak everything looked to him. Once again, he considered the idea he had been weighing for some time. The decision had been made, and this morning, solemnly, privately reconfirmed. Now that it was decided, and he knew he would at last end one search to embark upon another, he felt somewhat relieved. He turned and walked down the stairs to the gun cabinet. It was locked. Mary, his wife, had tried to keep it locked lately—but he knew where she kept the key. He found it. Quietly, he slipped the key into the lock and turned it, then pulled on the heavy door. It opened. He selected an expensive shotgun and removed it from the rack. It was an old favorite. He loaded it with care. Then he walked to his chair, lowered himself into it, and sat back. He removed one of his house slippers. Placing the cold steel gun barrel against his forehead, he carefully slipped his toe into the trigger guard and pressed down hard.

For Whom the Bell Tolls—On July 2, 1961, it tolled for Ernest Miller Hemingway, and was heard around the world.

CHAPTER 1

Some people feel that to be as famous as Ernest Hemingway automatically would bring them the happiness that comes with achievement, personal fulfillment, and financial reward. This may be true to a degree but, while Hemingway enjoyed being a writer, soldier of fortune, hunter, sailor, and fisherman—and being all of these extraordinarily well—he experienced many of the problems that beset us all.

From his earliest days, Ernest Hemingway was deeply into life. He loved stories about animals and nature. One of the first written works he cared for was a monthly serial titled *The Birds of Nature*. He also showed early signs of what many feel was his rich imagination by giving special "names" to animals and to his friends. (These are discussed later in the book.) He had keen observation of detail, even as a boy, and demonstrated remarkable memory. He was a strong and strong-willed youngster whose physical capabilities were to stand him in good stead until the latter days of his life. This is not to say that he did not experience times of substantial physical illness. However, generally, he proved to be stronger than most in body, will, determinism, and emotional drive.

His father, Clarence Edmonds Hemingway, was a graduate of Oberlin and held an M.D. degree from Rush Medical College in Chicago. A general practitioner with an ample patient following, "Ed" Hemingway was a large, muscular, barrel-chested man who stood six feet tall. He had met Grace Hall while they both were students at Oak Park High School in Oak Park, Illinois. They were married on October 1, 1896. Grace was small and slightly built, a music teacher who suffered from defective vision. It resulted from a siege of scarlet fever during her childhood and caused her to suffer frequent headaches. Both Ed and Grace were devout Christians. They worshipped regularly at the local Episcopal church.

Ernest was born July 21, 1899 and was baptized on October 1st, the Hemingways' third wedding anniversary. He was later described by his parents as a most delightful, though trying, frustrating, and sometimes disappointing, anniversary present. He was the second of six children and the oldest of two boys.

As he grew older, Ernest and his family often vacationed in the backwoods of Michigan, where he enjoyed spending considerable time with his grandfather. One of their favorite games was playing "Indians," with Ernest wearing a fanciful costume with fringed leggings. The death of his grandfather, in 1905, was a serious emotional trauma for young Ernest. He watched mutely as many of his grandfather's personal effects were burned in the backyard. Among them were jars from the attic in which snakes and other small creatures were preserved in alcohol. When thrown into the fire, they popped and shattered, and the alcohol flamed up. Jar after jar was tossed into the fire as they disposed of his grandfather's small wildlife collection. For the grief-stricken, terrified six-year-old, watching spellbound, the memory of it would be deeply fixed in his psyche. We love only to lose . . . and death must be surrounded by an aura of high drama, fire, and explosions—if we are to be worthy, if we are to be remembered as men.

Probably the greatest gift Dr. Hemingway gave to Ernest and his other children was an appreciation and love of nature. Ernest learned from him how to build fires, cook, and do various outdoor chores, including cleaning fish for the frying pan over an open fire. Also instilled in young Ernest was the need for the efficient care of rods and tackle, as well as the various types of rifles and shotguns around the Hemingway home. Ernest also learned from his father some of the basics of physical endurance. Dr. Hemingway cultivated an element of individualism in the boy which he always remembered in this outdoorsman role. In fact, the outdoors aspect of his identification with his father soon almost totally replaced his perception of Dr. Hemingway as a whole person. His father's interests, pastimes, idiosyncrasies, and values became fuzzy in Ernest's mind and merged with this more unrealistic outdoorsman image.

Ernest never could compete with his father in terms of his classical middle-class, Protestant ethic behavior, which included such dreary concepts as work for the sake of work, scholarship for the sake of getting ahead, and strongly-championed (and, for the most part, achieved) lofty moral standards. This exemplified the characteristic *superego* type of behavior which was so prevalent in Ernest's mother and father. (This is discussed in later pages.)

The early emphasis on outside activities, which included knowledge of game behavior, hunting techniques, and physical endurance, had a profound effect on Ernest. From his very earliest days, he was most interested in outdoor activity of an adventurous nature, much more so than other children his age, and that comparison invites a speculation: that this kind of early childhood life, this almost isolated, self-reliant type of behavior, built an *id* pattern of responses in Ernest since he was dealing with and reacting to his feelings with animal actors, not human peers, in his scenarios. He was successful in such a behavior pattern; therefore, he gravitated to this particular style for ego identification and support throughout life.

Most of the traveling Ernest did as a young schoolboy consisted of annual treks to Michigan. He had many early outdoor experiences, including fishing for mackerel and sea bass when the family vacationed one summer on Nantucket Island. During that holiday off the New England coast, Ernest went swimming daily, and developed a fascination with the ocean that was to endure for the rest of his life. In fact, this vacation kindled in him a love for the sea which culminated in two books, the first of which won him world acclaim—*The Old Man and The Sea*. The second was *Islands In the Stream*.

As Ernest entered the sixth grade, there was increased discussion in the family about plans for his becoming a doctor. The talk, however, was mainly between the two physicians in Ernest's family—his father and his Uncle Will.

The young Hemingway enjoyed dramatizing almost every type of story. He delighted in making up fantasies in which, invariably, he emerged as a hero's hero. He was easily persuaded, in March, 1912, to play Robin Hood in a seventh-grade production. Ernest cut quite a fanciful figure, wearing high-buckled shoes and a velvet cap, and carrying a homemade longbow. Dr. and Mrs. Hemingway continued to influence their son subtly toward church-oriented activities, planning for his spiritual future, while Ernest continued to indulge his greater love for exploring, swimming, and hiking—passions that were to persist throughout his life. He learned from his father that he should do things properly and well, if at all. This included outdoor sports as well as manual labor. In the latter, however, the boy took little pleasure.

Ernest coined a maxim, "afraid of nothing," and this became a behavior model which he affected no matter what the adversity nor what the challenge. His father had substantial influence in this "afraid of nothing" concept, as he strongly endorsed a high code of physical endurance and courage. This standard tied in beautifully with the love of hunting, fishing, and the general outdoors which was always so important to the senior Hemingway and which he instilled in Ernest.

Dr. and Mrs. Hemingway were very pleased that their son asserted his independence by delivering newspapers, shoveling snow, and taking on other chores in the community to supplement his weekly allowance. It was important to the Hemingways that Ernest embrace the highest Christian ideals, and he became a pillar of the Plymouth League for Young People. He also developed an interest in football and, in the fall of 1915, was a substitute tackle on a lightweight football team. This led to his first experience in dieting, for he had to maintain his weight at 135 pounds in order to qualify for this rugged, satisfyingly masculine game. It was at this point in his life that Ernest also became somewhat more interested in scholarly activities, such as learning ancient history and Latin, though he continued to prefer shooting and outdoor sports to studying. In athletics, he seemed to turn away from organized team sports, preferring individual physical activities to those that required group interaction and group competition.

Ernest had done a great deal of farm work during the summers between school semesters and had developed into a rather large, muscular, healthy young man. As a result of his size, he also became something of a bully and occasionally would intimidate his friends of the same age. During this time, his parents and other adults saw him as being "pushy" because of his aggressive nature. This aggressiveness led him, in 1916, to become highly interested in boxing. Later in life, he would relish telling stories of how his poor vision in his left eye had been caused by boxing injuries when he was a young man. It was in this type of storytelling, with its hyperbole, that he built his ego. His character had a distinctly flamboyant side which was as real as his modest side.

At about this time, Ernest's long-time desire to write emerged, and he became a reporter for *The Trapeze*, his high school's weekly newspaper. His first reporting effort described a performance by the Chicago Symphony. Ernest's teenage years were well-rounded and included studying, reporting on various events for the high school paper, and boxing, as well as boating and camping trips he enjoyed along the Des Plaines River.

The influence of his family, particularly his father, continued to be strong. On one occasion, Ernest asked his father what the term "masher" meant, after reading a newspaper story about someone who had been arrested for such behavior. In a form of defensive reaction, the elder Hemingway described it as a most heinous crime. He then heated up to a lecture on morals, condemning masturbation by declaring that it produced blindness, insanity, and death. He summed this up with the statement that prostitutes have venereal disease and that persons should keep their hands to themselves. This reflected his father's inability to talk reasonably about such matters, proscribed by his strict middle-class Victorian values and his upbringing. The episode also was a strong indication of Dr. Hemingway's super-ego orientation.

Once Ernest graduated from high school, he was faced with three choices: to go to work, to war (World War I), or to college. To the great disappointment of his parents, especially his father, he rejected college. He decided to go to work for the *Kansas City Star* instead, as soon as a position was available. He saw this as the route to asserting his independence and manhood. Though he had had a happy, and even an adventurous, childhood, he was eager to escape from under the thumb of his father, whose totally moral approach to life often had caused problems between them, especially when Ernest's behavior did not meet with his paternal parent's approval. Dr. Hemingway usually was quick to let Ernest know when his moral sensibilities had been offended. The boy, like his mother, often would "pen up" hostile feelings until he exploded in anger. Recalling his relationship with his father, Ernest later said that, on more than one occasion, he had surreptitiously aimed a gun at his father's head, when the latter's gaze was averted, and had fantasized the results of pulling the trigger.

Ernest could not stand displays of what he perceived as less than masculinity on the part of men. When his father told him goodbye at the train station as Ernest was leaving for Kansas City, Dr. Hemingway's eyes grew moist with tears, and he flavored the occasion with religious overtones as he kissed his son farewell. Ernest was embarrassed by the display and, for the first time, he felt that he was a stronger, more mature person than his father. He later recounted this incident in *For Whom The Bell Tolls* as he described a similar scene at a railroad station.

When Ernest went to work on the *Star,* he spent a great deal of time talking with the reporters about the approaches they used in getting their information and how they wrote their stories. He was particularly impressed with a reporter named Lionel C. Moise. Ernest had begun to define style and qualities in writing and writers, and he came to like Moise very much for his style and flair. The veteran journalist was an argumentative, fast-working, hard-drinking, forceful man who had a great way with words. He was a big man with thick, heavy fingers, but, in spite of this, his fingers flew as he pecked out news stories on the typewriter. Ernest heard many intriguing stories about him and his adventures with women. Clearly, Moise projected a fascinating masculine model of confidence and self-assurance with which the impressionable young reporter could identify, and would later emulate.

Ernest had begun to write sketches of people he met as a reporter. He was particularly interested in individuals who seemed daring and off-color. His writings also focused on men and women who were coping with alcoholism or drug problems. One of his early stories described a neurotic young boy who emasculated himself in an effort to become pious. This can be interpreted as a psychological statement by Hemingway rejecting his father's restrictive values with regard to sex and religion. This also was the first statement of an underlying psychological set that would predispose Ernest to suicide. The emasculation can be viewed as a symbolic suicide, for it marks the death of maleness in the young man who was the central character of his story.

During this period, Ernest attempted to develop his writing skills. He became interested in the war raging overseas and decided he should go to Europe to observe it firsthand. The decision was made over the strong objections of his father, who tried in every way to keep Ernest from going abroad. The lure of adventure, the prospect of crossing the Atlantic greatly excited Ernest. He had worked for the *Kansas City Star* for six months when he left for Europe and the war.

CHAPTER **2**

In Europe, Hemingway served as an ambulance driver for the Red Cross. He also was director of an emergency campaign in Northern Italy. He mixed freely with the Italian officers and became engrossed in the war activity. Talk of it soon grew into a hungry obsession.

He got his first look at the bizarre spectacle of gross human death soon after midnight one night when the Austrian troops across the river fired one of their missiles. Ernest heard it coming, and its shrill whine both frightened and excited him. The missile, on target all the way, exploded on contact nearby, killing large numbers of soldiers and wounding others. Ernest raced forward. He lifted a wounded Italian soldier and had carried him some 50 yards, when, suddenly, he felt a burst of pain. Ernest had taken a machine gun bullet in his right leg at the knee. Moments later, a second explosion buried 200 pieces of shrapnel in his back. He staggered forward. He was covered with blood, that of the Italian he was carrying mingled with his own. Later, when he was laid on the ground among the dead and dying, he experienced the feeling that dying was a very normal type of activity. He also realized, while lying there, that he was among the majority, for the dying and dead outnumbered those who had escaped harm. The experience was an exhilarating one for Hemingway. He had attempted to save the life of an unknown Italian soldier, and he knew that, by carrying the man to an ambulance, he had acquitted himself as well. In his first encounter with violent death, he had met danger, endured agony, and behaved manfully. He was a real hero, and one who had been badly wounded in the test of courage, to boot. All this, at 18 years of age.

Ernest, seriously injured, enjoyed exceptional care at the hands of the Italian medics. As he began to recuperate, he became more and more playful, jesting and joking with the orderlies and nurses. It was during this stay in the hospital that he met Agnes

CHAPTER 2

Hannah von Kurowsky, a beautiful nurse seven years his senior. Ernest wanted to get well quickly, not only for his own sake, but so he might pursue and win Agnes. He had fallen deeply in love with her.

Hemingway was the first American to be wounded in the campaign in Italy, and many people were interested in him and his recovery. One of them was Enrico Serena, an Italian. They became friends in the hospital, and later, Serena became the prototype for Captain Rinaldi, the surgeon in Hemingway's *A Farewell to Arms*.

Though Ernest had suffered terribly, he also enjoyed, to a considerable extent, this first personal encounter with severe physical injury. He had been wounded through both knees and had suffered more than 200 flesh wounds. He was eager to let his friends in America know about the extent of his injury and how well had had conducted himself under fire. He also was eager to tell them about the honor the Italians had bestowed upon him— the rank of second lieutenant. This was an undeniable badge which confirmed his manhood, his bravery, and his independence.

As he moved toward recovery, Hemingway enjoyed more and more the attention with which he was showered. Many visitors came to see him and to praise his heroism. He spared no detail in describing, at great length, the attack he had gone through—and his sufferings. Throughout it all, he projected masculinity, courage, and an ebullient good nature. His recovery was highlighted by the considerable attention he was receiving from both men, who offered hero worship, and women, equally attracted by his status as a war hero. Such adulation greatly added to his blossoming self-confidence. It was a maturing experience for him; he liked being attractive to women and respected by men.

Soon, Ernest was released from the hospital. After dating Agnes for a short time, he acknowledged to her that he was deeply in love with her. Later, he even talked of marrying her. However, Agnes was more mature and experienced than he, and realized the romance was fated to be only a fleeting involvement.

Ernest continued to recover from his wounds. Yet, in one revealing sidelight, he refused to appear in public until stripes, indicating he had been wounded in battle, were attached to his uniform. He objected to being considered anything other than a hero by the Italians. This early experience of adulation from others, coupled with his own great ego needs, laid the groundwork for a style of personal functioning embodying a self-centeredness that was to stamp his personality for the rest of his life. Agnes was to be immortalized as the nurse in Hemingway's *A Farewell to Arms*. Years later, after she married, she and her husband, Mr. Stanfield, were to live in Key West, Florida, where Ernest owned a home.

Ernest saw and wrote about a great deal of human suffering and death during the war. He began to tell himself, and others, that he had achieved special insights into the meanings of death and heroism. He seemed to be trying to convey the impression that to die was easy, yet he probably did not believe this. He had a fear of death and a fear of failure that were as profound as they were difficult to separate. For the rest of his life, Hemingway seemed to need to stay close to suffering and death in his personal relationships and his experiences, perhaps feeling that this closeness, even kinship, might diminish his fears of death and failure. However, he was never to achieve this freedom from fear. He constantly attempted to prove his courage by seeking to overcome specific physical limitations and to leap the hurdles of life, and by living at an artificial level of exuberance. For, if he let down, if he relaxed, he might see the specter. Waiting.

CHAPTER 3

There is a quotation from Shakespeare's *Henry IV* whose words moved Ernest deeply. He was never to forget the lines: "By thy troth, I care not; a man cannot die but once; we owe God a debt . . . and let it go which way it will, he that dies this year is quit for the next."

His experiences in Northern Italy would mean much to Ernest throughout his life. He had been seriously wounded and had taken five months to convalesce. During this time, he had had his first intense love affair. This momentous experience, coupled with the physical aspects of sickness and proximity to death itself, did much to mature him and shape his philosophy of life.

In the winter of 1919, Ernest traveled to Toronto, Canada, where he resumed writing newspaper copy. During the ensuing months, he sold some 15 articles to the *Weekly Star Magazine,* for which he was paid less than $150.00 for the lot. His major gratification, though, was seeing his name in print. He also enjoyed the idea of being paid on a contractual basis, for writing rather than searching out magazines which might be interested in publishing his work, but only on speculation. After working in Toronto for a short period, Ernest returned to Michigan, lured by the prospect of seeing old friends again and enjoying some hunting and fishing. He shared a room with a friend in the large apartment of Mr. and Mrs. Y. K. Smith.

It was at the Smiths' apartment that Ernest first met Hadley Richardson. He was at once enormously attracted to her. He also came to have a great respect for her stability and maturity. He was to marry her the following summer, and be influenced by her throughout the rest of his life.

After their marriage, Ernest contracted with *The Toronto Star* to write articles and stories, which were to be dispatched to the newspaper via the mail. He was to be paid space rates for all of the material the newspaper used. The agreement with the *Star* also stipulated that he was to be reimbursed for all expenses incurred in writing the articles, including travel costs, and that there was no limitation on where he could travel. This provision enabled Ernest and Hadley to go to Paris, where, in those days, they were able to live modestly but comfortably until he began to receive money from the *Star* for his articles and stories. Supplementing these writing funds was the trust income Hadley received from an inheritance.

From Hadley, Ernest received a great deal of love and enthusiasm, both invaluable in nourishing his ever-demanding ego structure. His marriage to Hadley thus was a major fundamental step in Ernest's psychological evolution. She provided the essential vehicle by which he reinforced his sometimes flagging concept of his masculinity, adequacy, and independence. Hadley's almost totally uncritical, positive regard, her undisguised respect and adoration supported Ernest's sense of identity and self-confidence and provided much of his motivation to explore and further develop his capabilities. Had she been devaluing, or even less enthusiastic, Ernest might not have matured as a writer of Pulitzer Prize and Nobel Prize stature.

The Hemingways took a small apartment on *Rue du Cardinal Lemoine* in Paris and began to meet and associate with many interesting members of the Parisian art colony. Among their new friends were Sherwood Anderson, a writer from the Midwestern United States; Gertrude Stein; Alice B. Toklas; Ezra Pound; and other gifted artists and writers, as well as many who were attempting to become artists and writers.

All his life Hemingway dearly loved being where the action was, and Paris certainly was the place to be during the postwar years. He quickly explored the terrain outside Paris and found the countryside impressive. However, he had never liked bad weather, and the Paris rains were depressing to him. But he enjoyed his newspaper work and met many leaders who had been on both sides of the war effort. This was an exciting and invigorating time for him. Being an outdoorsman and sportsman, he thoroughly enjoyed being able to do some fishing in the Rhone Valley. However, there was one drawback: throughout his stay in Paris and Northern Europe he was continually beset with viral infections and throat difficulties.

In July, 1923, Ernest published *Three Stories and Ten Poems*. The book actually was printed, rather than published, and originally there were only 300 copies available. Soon after this book came out, Ernest and Hadley left for Canada. Hadley was six months pregnant, and they wanted to be certain the child would be either a Canadian or a United States citizen. Their first child,

John Hadley Nicanor Hemingway, was born on October 10, 1923. Ernest was quite apprehensive about being a father, afraid that he was too young. He experienced what many fathers feel on the birth of their first child—the realization that they no longer can avoid the full responsibility of adulthood, and the bittersweet dread that some of the good times associated with total freedom may be gone forever. Three months later, in January, 1924, Ernest and Hadley decided to return to Europe—much to the distress of Ernest's parents. They wanted "Bumby," as their new grandchild affectionately was called, to remain as close as possible. But Ernest was determined. He also was looking forward to the release of *In Our Time,* which was to be published in a limited number of copies within the next few weeks.

The young couple returned to Paris. They secured an inexpensive apartment on *Rue Notre Dame des Champs.* This was another good period in Hemingway's life. His book, *In Our Time,* had been released and was selling well, proving to him his ability to write in other than a journalistic setting. In addition, he was able to indulge his wanderlust rather freely during 1925. Since he was a keen observer, travel rounded out his education. During 1925, he traveled extensively in Scotland and England and spent considerable time in Spain with his good friend John Dos Passos. In Spain, he strengthened his ties with Dos Passos. He also developed an overwhelming passion for bullfighting, becoming a true *aficionado.* This was totally predictable since Ernest Hemingway was constantly striving for masculinity, and bullfighting was a patently masculine activity. He regarded men who did not like bullfighting as less than masculine. From this we can understand the rationale behind Hemingway's strong and fervent support for all aspects of the sport and his violent opposition to any attempts by its critics to mitigate or soften it.

With the publication of his third book, *The Torrents of Spring,* Hemingway made a valiant effort to explain to his parents why he had written his fourth book, *The Sun Also Rises,* soon to be released. Throughout his adult life, it had been a great personal tragedy to him that his parents neither appreciated nor understood his writings and, in fact, were disdainful of most of them. This created great problems between Ernest and his parents and caused undercurrents of emotional distress throughout much of the little time they had together. For a person with such an expansive ego as Hemingway, the difficulty in explaining his writings to his parents was enormous and emotionally draining. He would become irate with either of them at even the idea of having to explain his work.

His mother, in particular, had put him on the defensive

concerning his choice of subject matter for *The Sun Also Rises*, as well as his treatment of it. The book—filled with impotence, impenitence, promiscuity, drinking, and aimless, unproductive characters and lives—offended her. Ernest tried to convince her that a writer should not have to defend his choice of material, but must justify only the method he uses to treat it. He tried to explain to her that he had described, as well as anyone could, those characters later to be so vividly remembered by all who have read his books.

When viewed through personality structure, the family conflict over Ernest's writing was inevitable. Being more *id*-oriented, Ernest described the *id*-oriented aspects of man—his more basic drives, such as those for sex, dominance over others, material possessions, food, and comfort. These were aspects of realism his parents could never understand, much less accept. Their *superego* personality structure required more high-minded literature. Their lives personified a striving to ignore or overcome the animalistic qualities and drives of mankind. Literature, to them, was intended to set an example of the lifestyle man *should* live. They felt it should be uplifting, rather than describe intolerable qualities, sordid behavior, and degrading conditions. For these reasons, the older Hemingways must have felt, on many occasions, the need to make excuses, even to apologize, to their Oak Park, Illinois friends and neighbors for their son's choices of subjects and plots.

Ernest tried desperately to get his mother and father to understand that he was writing about life and people as they are—real people with weaknesses as well as strengths. He was writing about life experiences, he told them, and if some persons were accusing him of using his talents only for sensationalism, and to make money, then so be it.

One reason for Ernest's interpersonal problems is rooted in his ego drive. According to egopsychology, the personality has three parts: the *superego,* the *id,* and the *ego.* The superego represents the social and cultural demands of society. Some psychologists characterize the superego as the conscience of the individual.

The second part of the personality, the id, consists of the basic animal impulses of the individual, whose aggressiveness comes from the strength of the id. The id represents the more animalistic and primitive part of man. The id and superego, as one can readily see, are in direct conflict with one another. The id says "I want" and "I demand." The superego is concerned with what society wants, what the culture demands.

The third part of the personality, the ego, has the responsibility of satisfying both the id and the superego. A healthy, well-integrated personality has a strong ego which is able to meet the demands of the superego as well as those that derive from id impulses. An individual whose ego structure is weak and leans toward the drive of the superego is apt to be a perfectionist. Such a person often manifests great religiosity, is primarily concerned with what is right regardless of his feelings, and is motivated to do "right" no matter what personal sacrifice or pain it entails.

On the other hand, an individual whose weak ego causes his personality scales to be unbalanced in favor of the id is one who is seen as "spoiled," one who is very aggressive and strives for self-aggrandizement. Such an individual is interested primarily in himself, fulfilling only his own needs; he is concerned with the environment meeting *his* demands, regardless of the needs of others. This kind of person functions independently rather than interdependently. An id-oriented person is one who is motivated to do those things that are personally satisfying, regardless of the personal pain and sacrifice he must endure in terms of the societal and cultural censure that may result from his actions. From the psychodiagnostic clues we have seen, Ernest Hemingway would seem to be this id-oriented sort of person. This orientation accounts for much of his behavior, as is revealed most clearly in his writings.

A source of many of Ernest Hemingway's emotional stresses was his relationship with his parents. His mother and father were almost completely superego-oriented. They were seriously concerned with what they should do, what their children should do, what was "right," what was expected of them, and what was expected of their children. They inculcated in their children concerns about the restraints of society and the social order. This inculcation, or inoculation, did not "take" with Ernest. He rejected this superego model. He could never sacrifice his wants or desires for the sake of societal expectations. Ernest Hemingway's id-orientation was diametrically opposed to the personality makeup of his parents. Had he accepted their superego role model, his life would have been completely different. He would have channeled his high motivation to achieve into different areas. If he *had* become a writer, most certainly his subject matter and style would have been different; he would have had a less unorthodox life style; and there is a possibility he would not have committed suicide, since his actions would have been predicated on what was "right." He never would have embarked on the sanguine flight from responsibility which suicide represents.

The superego-orientation can maintain, and even sustain, some personalities—occasionally converting to a crystallized martyr complex when the saps of temptation cease to flow. Unconscious masters of sublimation, denial, rationalization, or reaction formation, martyrs receiving their payoff from the "I've always been a shining example" game are reluctant to self-destruct, especially so long as they can entrap a listener. For the id oriented, the ebbing of hormones, the declining functioning of organs, the tyranny of years, and the fleetness and fickleness of nubile prey can lead to morose musings.

Of course, ironic exceptions occur in life, as well as psychology: Ernest's superego-oriented father, Dr. Hemingway, ended his own life.

CHAPTER 4

As may be expected, the fundamental incongruence in personality orientation and the dissonance between lifestyles created considerable tension in Hemingway familial relations. While Ernest was a source of pride to his parents, he also was a wellspring of confusion, hurt, and shame. He failed to live up to many of the expectations of his mother and father, who, in turn, failed to nourish many of their son's deep needs by withholding their unqualified approval.

His parents saw Ernest's failure as stemming from his rejection of their lifestyle. He failed to complete his formal education by not attending college. He did not prepare himself to assume a professional role in the community. To his parents, writing was not a profession and particularly not when it produced the type of works their son was writing. Because of their strong, rigid consciences, his writing caused them shame and embarrassment.

On the other hand, Ernest felt his parents deserted him when they were unable to provide the ego support, recognition, and affection he felt was due him on the publication of his first book. He never understood why his parents were so adamantly opposed to what he was writing. He was hurt and alienated by their open rejection not only of his style, but of the content of his work. Writing had become the *raison d'etre* for Ernest; it was the only "safe," solid, common ground on which he felt that he and his parents could maintain a close relationship. When this common ground did not materialize, the relationships within the family disintegrated. No longer were they as close as they could have been, or once had been. Interestingly, the superego structure of the parents was so strong that it took precedence over their desire to nourish the warm, close, loving relationship which they felt was proper and necessary between parents and child.

As mentioned elsewhere, the values adhered to by his parents were obviously so wrong as goal models for Ernest that he justified his rejection of these values through the productivity and creativity of his life. While his parents tried to instill in Ernest what they saw as typical, middle-class American values, he rejected these as being too confining for him and adopted a much freer life style, one whose lack of structure was much more satisfying to him. When his productivity and creativity waned, however, his value structure started to crumble—ultimately pointing to the decision to end his existence.

In his relationship with his parents, as well as with his friends, Hemingway often was characterized as having high integrity. Even when plagued with family and personal problems, he attempted to communicate with significant persons in his life on a basic level of honesty and openness. To him, straightforward communication was not only the banner of his growth and development, but it indicated his constant searching for a deeper understanding of his motivations and ways of thinking.

He was so enamored of life and intense about life—especially writing, boxing, hunting, fishing, drinking, and interpersonal relationships—that he added depth and a sense of humor to all of these experiences, not only for himself, but for those who were associated with him. Those who were in his company often looked to him to set the level of their expectations for whatever activity was occurring or about to occur. He was handsome and extremely pleasant and very much alive. When happy, he often sang, danced a little jig, or shadowboxed; in short, he was at times delightfully effervescent. He also was highly opinionated, one who decided what was right for him (without considering long the needs of others) and often proceeded on that basis.

He always looked at marriage as something of an interference with the many things he wished to do—writing, hunting, fishing, boxing, seeing other women, or myriad other possibilities. He was hostile in reference to the bonds of marriage and conceded that, while a man gained from (and needed to be married to) a woman he loved, he also lost considerably in terms of his freedom. This is understandable, since marriage is more an institution of the superego in our culture than of the id. In *The Snows of Kilimanjaro*, he obliquely described himself as "the cock crowing on the dunghill of love."

It is interesting that Hemingway has been described as articulate. According to some, however, he would try three or four times to say many of the things he wanted to say. Some of his close associates also noticed that he had a slight speech impediment, a difficulty in pronouncing the letter *L*. At the same time, he had little tolerance for any kind of mediocrity or incapacity in others, and even less in himself. This rejection of any personal imperfection could easily have led to his compensatory striving for status through creativity; but it also could have added a dimension of peevishness to the usually pleasant Ernest. He was a taker rather than a giver. True, he gave intensely in some human relationships. But he required such indulgences that friendships and romances, including marriages, were greatly strained and frequently torn asunder.

On numerous occasions, he freely characterized friends or other close associates in his stories. It did not seem to bother him that these characters were only slightly camouflaged. There is a case of his writing about a fat girl who had gone to Paris to study piano and, hopefully, to have a love affair. After being in Paris for more than a year, she was still a virgin. He wrote how she would listen through the wall of her apartment to the sounds of others while they made love. The character, in real life, was a girl who happened to be a close friend of Hadley, his wife. She was easily identifiable in the story to those who knew her. It was a poignant example of how Hemingway's self-centeredness took precedence over other considerations. He used people for his own needs and purposes. If he had to forfeit a friendship or a romance in doing so, then so be it. The fulfillment of his needs was the primary objective.

The fact that Hemingway could be exceedingly cruel and harsh to those he had previously loved, or with whom he had close relationships, is exemplified well in *The Snows of Kilimanjaro*, in which, portraying himself as Harry, he berates Harry's wife, accusing her of destroying his talent and calling her a rich person who can provide only the funds to finance his existence. He even accuses her of not allowing him to work and of betraying him with other lovers, which was a projection of course of his own behavior. Harry also said that he would like to destroy his wife in bed. This could be indicative of the extremes of Hemingway's hatred for women, and for all persons upon whom he had to be dependent. He was particularly dependent upon his second wife, Pauline Pfeiffer, for her money.

Hemingway was a pragmatist and, while writing for money as well as enjoyment, he manipulated his material in the ways that would make it most saleable. He once made the statement that the advantage of *In Our Time* over E. E. Cummings's *The Enormous Room* (which did not sell) was that everyone could read *In Our Time* with enjoyment. Persons of high intellect would enjoy the idea, he noted, and those with less intelligence could enjoy following the story. He wrote so that any reader with a tenth-grade education could understand his works without difficulty.

Ernest wanted very much to be his own man in his writing as well as in his physical activities. His anger flared when it was said that his career had been overly influenced by Sherwood Anderson or Gertrude Stein. While he did acknowledge his debt to Anderson, he became incensed at the credit for his accomplishments given to Gertrude Stein, feeling that all she had done was suggest he go into writing novels and abandon newspaper work.

Hemingway and Gertrude Stein had a running love/combat relationship going for years. It embodied elements that most psychologists deal with frequently: ambivalence, in which love and hate vie alternately for dominance in a relationship; and sibling rivalry, wherein children in a family try to outperform one another in competition for approval (love) from the figures in authority (parents). As grown "children," related by profession rather than blood, Hemingway and Stein vacillated, publicly and privately, between mutual adoration and mutual contempt. Through their work, they sought the approval of the bestowers of grace (the public), whose favor, manifested by little purchases massed together, granted the recognition, fame and life style these ambivalent protagonists required. In kind moments, Ernest spoke highly of Gertrude's gifts—and their public and private banter held hidden springs of a sexual attraction that Ernest indicated, years later, had never been consummated. In a letter, he said Gertrude had learned to write dialogue from him, and he, to write "rhythms in prose" from her. Before he could admit to this, however, Hemingway had to grow, to mellow—and Gertrude Stein had to die.

Bullfighting, to Hemingway, was the ultimate of physical risk, the full range of the saga of life and death—pure vicarious enjoyment at its best. In addition to his ardor for the bullfights, he loved Spain, with its wonderful countryside and people, so much that it could have been his homeland. In June, 1925 he, Hadley, and a number of friends moved to Pamplona, establishing themselves in the Hotel Quintana. The matadors often stayed in the same hotel. This was most satisfactory to Hadley, since she also enjoyed the bullfights. One aspect of the fights which Ernest loved was that of observing the reactions of other spectators. He seemed fascinated that some people appeared horrified while others cheered. He thoroughly enjoyed comparing them, one with another.

Both Hadley and Ernest were particularly enamored of the bullfighter named Ordoñez. Ernest decided to make him the hero of a novel he was writing at the time called *Fiesta*, which later was to become *Death in the Afternoon*. In this book, which was published by Scribner's in 1932 and dedicated by Hemingway to Pauline Pfeiffer (then his wife), he concentrated on human living and dying. Since bullfighting involves intense, overwhelming emotion, he was able to apply his keen observational abilities to an in-depth study of coping, confrontation, and risk-taking behavior. The bullring enabled him to observe violent death firsthand and, as he stated, there was no better opportunity to see it since there were no wars to cover at the time.

In attempting to explain the morality of the bullfight, Hemingway said that *moral behavior* is that form of behavior after which one feels good, while that after *immoral behavior* one feels bad. Hemingway made a questionable observation in *Death in the Afternoon* when explaining the cruelty to horses in the bullring. People who identify with animals, he says, such as lovers of dogs, cats, horses, whatever, are capable of greater cruelty to human beings than people who do not identify with animals.

It is interesting that Hemingway defends the killing of horses during the bullfight by portraying them as more like birds than horses, after describing their heads, long legs, and necks covered by the canvas. He cites in great detail how the horses are gutted by the horns, and a single horse dangling, impaled on the horns of the bull. He also was opposed to efforts by the Spanish government to require that the abdomens of the horses be protected by the wearing of mattress covers. Ernest saw this as a suppression. He claimed that the agony of the unprotected horses killed was less than that of the horses gored while wearing the mattress covers. He maintained that the protective covering would fail to reduce the level of pain suffered by the horses. Hemingway called the horses' deaths "a comic tragedy" and seems almost defensive in his lengthy eloquence justifying cruelty for the sake of the beauty of the emotion and physical trauma of the bullfight. He virtually attacks anyone who does not "love the bullfight" as lacking full appreciation for what he calls the "tragedy and ritual of the fight." A person who does not have this appreciation is limited, he implies, saying that a person either has it or does not have it. This single-minded equation of the "full life" with bullfighting is an example of his drive for justifying and proving his masculinity.

Hemingway showed his gift for analogy in comparing the mystique of bullfighting with the drinking of wine; both, he said, are to be savored with great appreciation. He called wine one of the most civilized of the world's offerings, as well as one of the most natural. Brought to great perfection, it offers a vast range of enjoyment, as much as or more than any other sensory pleasure which can be bought. He said that one's appreciation of wine, like one's appreciation of the bullfight, can increase with time and experience.

It is significant that Hemingway so thoroughly enjoyed the

bullfight, which represents a rather one-sided win for the man. While bullfighters may be injured or even killed, the bull never stands a chance to live past the fight. Nor is a bull allowed to fight more than once in the ring. After the contest, if he has won, he is destroyed. Thus, he dies, if not by the matador's sword, then after the fight.

Ernest's keen observation of people and cultures is demonstrated in *Death in the Afternoon* in his descriptions of the personalities and fighting styles of the bullfighters. In a quasi-psychological manner, he describes in colorful detail the personal aspects of the fighters. He speculates about how courage would smell if it had an odor, comparing it with the smell of a "frozen road" or with "a wave when the wind rips the top from it." He also compares cultural patterns of the English and French regarding death and killing with those of the Spanish. The English kill only for sport, he explains, and the French kill only for their cooking pots, while the Spanish have the inherent pride which makes them feel worthy to give what he calls the "gift of death." Hemingway pointed out that, in some regions of Spain, bullfighting is not in vogue and is of no interest to the people. He said that, for people of a region or country to love bullfights, bulls must be raised in their area, and they must have an interest in death as well. The English and French live for life, he said, but in some areas of Spain, people are more accustomed to death: owing to their dangerous occupations, the concept of death has no revulsion for them.

In *Death in the Afternoon*, Hemingway identified closely with the Spanish people who enjoy the bullfight. He was extravagant in his efforts to justify his, and their, interest in watching the spectacle of death. He philosophized about it, describing the bullfight as an opportunity to see death being offered as a gift to be avoided or refused as well as accepted. All this could be seen in the afternoon for the price of a ticket. Hemingway seemed to be fostering the thesis that the study of death, through what occurred in the bullring, was a full justification for the "sport," symbolizing the struggle between man and the allegorical beasts he must fight. One wonders whether or not he was studying death, and evaluating his concepts and feelings about it, when he "gave" death as a gift, as he described doing to literally thousands of various types of animals, fish, and birds during his lifetime.

Hemingway was the most physical of the physical. Examples of this abound in his novels. He told stories about the whores of Spain who would not have sex with dwarfs or cripples. One story is related of a man who was normal, except for his legs, which were only six inches long. He told the whore that he was a man like any man, but the whore said, according to Hemingway, that he was not a man like other men and that was why she would not have sex with him.

Then there is the story of the duck whose throat had been cut by some Spaniards so that blood could be drained from its body for the making of gravy. The duck was stroked gently as it bled to death.

Other tales describe how mules' and donkeys' legs were broken and the animals shoved into shallow water to drown before the arrival of invading troops.

Hemingway also was capable of great affection and expressed his love of humanity in his writings. In *The Torrents of Spring*, he describes how Scripps picks up a frozen bird, close to death, which had fallen by the railroad tracks. He puts the bird inside his shirt and warms it. The small creature nestles close and pecks most appreciatively. To Hemingway, Scripps and the bird had a common enemy, the severe cold.

Hemingway did an enormous amount of drinking, and portrayed all of his important characters as constantly drinking or coming into contact with people who were. It would be interesting to make an accounting of the literally thousands of times, during his writings, in which he mentions drinking, being drunk, or the various ways of enjoying alcohol.

By 1925, Ernest had written (mostly in Paris) a book which was being called *The Torrents*. In it, he chastised his old friend, Sherwood Anderson, and then insulted Gertrude Stein by entitling Part IV "The Making and Marring of Americans." Everyone was opposed to his attempting to have this book published except Pauline Pfeiffer, who was enthusiastic about it. Ernest went against the best advice of his friend Dos Passos, and that of Hadley, in submitting the book for publication. Dos Passos had thought it was not quite good enough to be submitted, and Hadley felt it was detestable to chastise his close friend, Sherwood Anderson, in the work. This showed how difficult—and bullheaded—Hemingway could be in interpersonal relations, not listening to even those closest to him, but proceeding under his own steam to do whatever he wished.

Hemingway deeply loved chance-taking, risk, and danger. This seems to be what led him into his affair with Pauline Pfeiffer. He once described having an extra-marital affair as an enjoyable activity, one in which the lover both loves and hates, but lives the experience day by day, as in combat. In other words, he sought out involvements that were challenges not only to his physical safety, but to his emotional safety. Again, this is symptomatic of his continual striving to prove his adequacy and worth to himself.

The writings of Hemingway reflect a multifaceted personality. While he could be distressed with women and virtually hate them, he also described being unbelievably happy with women, as if he were drunk or crazy happy. This was characteristic of Hemingway in that he liked emotional highs and thrived on them. He did not do well with run-of-the-mill, routine, or average days; ordinary life was stultifying to his creative muse. To be productive, he sought emotional highs, through love experiences with women or physical confrontations with men. He could occasionally be deeply moved, however, by a simple, idyllic, naturalistic setting. The call of the kingfisher as it flew over the water, the squirrel chattering in the tree, the wind rustling through the branches, and the waiter's service in Chicotes in Madrid—all of these he described beautifully. The simple, or the profound, in human experience could set him emotionally aglow.

Hemingway's writings are filled with descriptions of gross experiences that evidently excited him. These include accounts of shooting a large crab between the eyes and watching it disintegrate, seeing crabs feeding on human bodies, observing animals which had been gunshot taking days to die, shooting sharks between the eyes, and the continuous slaughter of various types of birds and other animals, especially during African safaris.

He was a taker, and made no effort, so far as we know, to restore to any significant extent the wildlife which he so enjoyed killing. The animals, he felt, were there for the taking. Someone was bound to kill them, and he might as well be the one. This feeling seems to be exemplified in Dorothy's attitude toward fox coats, described in *The Fifth Column,* which required the slaughter of foxes for the making of the coats.

Hemingway projected his personality constantly in his novels to various degrees. He used the names of actual bars in his works, such as Chicotes in *The Fifth Column,* and only partially camouflaged many of his characters, including himself. He was a great admirer of the female physique and seemed to be a "leg man," often talking about long, smooth, straight legs.

The year 1926 found Hemingway visiting with Scott and Zelda Fitzgerald in Paris while attempting to finish his novel *The Sun Also Rises.* He also appeared to be in a considerable quandary about a young woman, Pauline Pfeiffer, who apparently had decided she was going to marry him. He was heavily involved in an affair with her at this time, and, though the relationship brought him great pleasure, it also caused some emotional pain. He loved Hadley, had great respect for her, and felt responsible for their son, Bumby. But Hemingway was a person of enormous physical appetites, as well, and one who craved to live life to its fullest. He could not withdraw from his new adventure with

CHAPTER 4

Pauline. In those days, he thought a great deal about fate and had ruminated about suicide and death. He was not totally serious at the time about taking his own life, but as his personal situation became more complicated and his sense of guilt increased, he saw suicide as a kind of interesting option that could lead to nothingness—to relaxation and relief. He also wondered what his level of courage would be when facing certain death. Most of these thoughts appear to have arisen from feelings of self-pity over having become so mired between adventure and duty.

It was in the early spring of 1926 that Hadley asked Ernest if he were in love with Pauline. He immediately turned the question against her, upbraiding her for having brought up the matter. By doing so, he sought to lift the burden of guilt from himself and place it on Hadley, thus bringing them closer to separation. It was a very difficult time for both of them; however, Ernest managed to write a great deal during this period in an effort to lose himself in his work and do something that could be considered worthwhile. It was during this time that he finished "Fifty Grand" and "Alpine Idyll." The latter story was bought by *Scribner's Magazine*. By the time he was ready to write the dedication for *The Sun Also Rises*, he and Hadley had separated. The event left Ernest bewildered. He could not accept the actuality of the breakup. He still loved Hadley and thought continually about the five years he had spent with her. *The Sun Also Rises* was to be his first novel. Yet writing its dedication did little to ease his feelings of remorse.

Early in life, Hemingway demonstrated his fatalism. Probably the most obvious indication of his feelings of emptiness and despair was his short story "A Clean Well-lighted Place." The depression echoed in this work is overpowering. A very safe game for psychologists to play is to make diagnostic predictions of behavior after observing the behavior. From the vantage point of today, it is obvious that we can analyze Ernest Hemingway's writings much more perceptibly than we could prior to the circumstances surrounding his death. Nevertheless, after reading "A Clean Well-lighted Place," one could safely predict the author was, and would continue to be, haunted by despair heightened by feelings and fears of failure. While a psychologist would have been on relatively shaky ground in predicting Hemingway's ultimate suicide from his early works, the therapist familiar with Hemingway through these writings would not be surprised to learn of his self-destruction.

Hadley told Ernest that, if he and Pauline would separate for 100 days, and then still wished to be together after that period of time, she would consent to divorce him. Ernest and Pauline decided the easiest way to accomplish this 100-day separation would be by Pauline's going to New York. She went, but she violated the spirit of the agreement by writing and telegramming him almost daily.

Her letters gave him some comfort, but they were not enough. She lavished praise on him, calling him "lovely," "smart," and "perfect," but he was miserable—miserable because he bore, in his own mind, the full weight of the breakup of his marriage, which he felt had been better than most. The only comfort he could give himself was to rationalize that things had been so good they had to get bad. He took the full blame for the problems between himself and Hadley, telling friends that he was living in a personal hell. He could not sleep, but he managed to continue to work. *Scribner's Magazine* had just bought "The Killers" for $200.00.

As time went on, Ernest became even more remorseful. He began to think seriously of taking his own life. Suicide, he felt, would spare Hadley the divorce procedure and eliminate him as a symbol of sin from Pauline's life. His religious beliefs haunted him; in the evenings he prayed for both women. He was tormented by conflicting feelings: he did not want to hurt Hadley but loved Pauline. He felt guilty, depressed, useless, and as if he were needlessly punishing those whom he loved and respected. His many complex feelings threatened to destroy his emotional balance and well-being. He was an aggressive person, and to his detriment at this time, he turned this aggressive drive upon himself. Psychologists generally agree that aggression turned inward converts to depression.

The fear of failure, depression, feelings of uselessness and impending doom plagued Hemingway throughout much of his life. Significantly, even after the praise and approbation heaped upon him for his heroism in the Italian campaign in World War I, Hemingway still had feelings of worthlessness. In 1920, when he was 21, he told his bride-to-be, Hadley, that he was seriously considering suicide. Feelings and thoughts of suicide apparently enticed Ernest Hemingway again and again throughout his entire adult life.

During this time of depression, he wrote "A Canary for One" and "In Another Country." The former was an account of his return journey from Antibes with Hadley that previous August. "In Another Country" was based on physical therapy sessions he received after being wounded in Italy and the conversations he had with an Italian major who had suffered a hand injury and whose wife had died of pneumonia. It was while he was working on this story that he received word from Hadley: She wanted him to move some of the furniture to her new apartment. Hemingway wept bitterly while carrying out this symbolic task for her. The moving of the furniture caused him great grief. As he took it to

Hadley's new residence, he must have asked himself whether or not his decision about Pauline was worth such emotional stress. Yet he persisted in the course of action he had chosen, in spite of the psychological pain involved. He knew he was flying in the face of all he had been taught about marital fidelity in his religious upbringing, but he wanted Pauline—wanted her enough to bring himself to the brink of suicide.

It should be noted that, while riding the crests, id-oriented people usually manage to avoid guilt feelings. But id, as driver, consumes more energy than most psyches can long maintain. When the driven lets up a moment to rest, and looks at what has been occurring, a crack can open in this carefree veneer, through which the vigilant superego may hastily discharge a dose of guilt in an effort to capture the personality. Id will not have this, of course; the breach will be patched, and the organism streaks off again on its quest, trailing the fading, noxious gas of the superego's failure. But superego is patient, and, the next time, may be more potent. Potent enough, perhaps, that id will be too tired to rally, not alert enough to spot the danger to the organism, and guilt, man's own creation, may inundate its creator. At such a time, a hand might reach for a bottle, repeatedly, for years, or for a gun, just once.

Ernest showed he was attempting to be man enough to carry the responsibility for the break-up of the marriage by carrying it totally on his shoulders. He told his friends that Hadley had done no wrong and that he was purely and simply a son-of-a-bitch. He also told some, including Scott Fitzgerald, about his suicidal feelings and that he felt he was not getting over them. He was open and sincere at a time that required openness and sincerity. In periods of extreme emotional stress, one can hardly take on further dishonest behavior of his own manufacture.

The sales of *The Sun Also Rises* were excellent at this time and gave Hemingway considerable hope for the future, shoring up his emotional defenses against his ominous, black thoughts.

But the book's success was not without an element of distress for its author. Dr. and Mrs. Hemingway disliked it. Grace Hemingway felt her son had lost all interest in honor and those other things in life she valued so highly. She could not understand why he had used vulgar words so often in his writings. And neither she nor her husband thought it was any distinction to produce what the *Literary Digest Book Review Magazine* had called a "sex novel." When they communicated these reactions to Ernest, he became very angry. He accused them of being disloyal to him and not understanding him. Again, he was deeply hurt by their reactions to one of his works, which was being called by some the finest novel of Hemingway's generation.

CHAPTER **5**

When the 100-day agreement ended, Pauline's ship docked at Cherbourg. She and Ernest immediately departed for a skiing vacation. Ernest was divorced from Hadley on January 27, 1927.

In writing *The Sun Also Rises*, Ernest had been very hard on a number of his friends and associates by describing them most unflatteringly in his pages. He seemed to get to know people well, after which they might well become characters in books, and only thinly disguised in the bargain. This caused great embarrassment and resentment among some of the friends and acquaintances described in his books, who wondered what they had done to invoke such mentions. Hemingway, in short, simply used people for his own purposes. He used even his intimate friendships and seemed, in fact, to be endeavoring to be the "son-of-a-bitch" he called himself.

During the months in 1927 when he was attempting to adjust to giving up his wife and child, he tried to conceal his troubled feelings from Pauline and others in various ways. He pretended to be bothered by rumors that certain "demented persons" who had read *The Sun Also Rises* were out "to get him." Here were the early signs of a paranoid-colored thought pattern which was to haunt him during the latter months of his life. During such times, those closest to him found him cold and self-absorbed, with little capacity for friendship. This was a very rough time for Hemingway in that he was having to adjust both to the loss of Hadley and to not seeing Bumby as often as he would like. At the same time, he was constantly under the gun from some of his friends—and former friends—who had been insulted by his characterizations of them in *The Sun Also Rises*.

By 1927, Hemingway had finished the manuscript of a new book which he called *Men Without Women*. From the title, it appears that he really was exploring whether or not men could live without women. In short, he was blaming women for his recent great sorrow. Even the fact that Hadley had been so outstanding a person only caused him to condemn women all the more. All of us must project blame elsewhere at times in order to live with ourselves, for few can bear the full weight of their own wrongdoings—fancied or real. Predictably, Ernest placed his blame on women, for a considerable time. Probably, at the end, these projections no longer served. Like everything else.

Within our culture, one measure of adjustment is the manner in which we interact and function with others. We have three clearly different choices. We can be essentially dependent upon others, essentially independent of others, or we can function interdependently. The most satisfying mode of adjustment is the interdependent role. In this lifestyle, the individual is concerned about not only his needs but about the needs of others. He acts mutually to fulfill his needs and those of others in his environment. The dependent person is concerned only about his particular needs and adopts the dependent lifestyle: thus, he sees others in his environment as there to satisfy his needs. This dependent personality has little or no concern about fulfilling the needs of others.

The person who adopts an independent lifestyle also has little or no concern about the needs of others. In this respect, the strongly independent person has much in common with the dependent person. His prime objective is fulfillment of his own needs, regardless of the emotional cost to others. Hemingway was one of the most rigid adherents of this individualistic lifestyle. Rarely, if ever, did he function on an emotionally interdependent level of adjustment, at which the most fulfilled, content, and mentally healthy seem to operate. This explains, to great measure, some of his seemingly inexplicable behavior, which many laymen feel totally lacked credibility. Though some of his actions still remain enigmatic, when we observe his adoption of the independent lifestyle, they become less puzzling.

While trying to justify the writing of *The Sun Also Rises* to his parents, Hemingway also gave them the news of his separation from Hadley. He told his parents that Hadley and their son, Bumby, were doing very well and that he had turned over to them all of the profits from his book, which, at that time, was in its fifth printing.

Thus, 1927 found Ernest being divorced by Hadley, planning to marry Pauline Pfeiffer, and working on the book *Men without Women*. Also during this period, he was able to reconstruct a relationship with his parents to some degree. He made great efforts to explain, to his father in particular, his divorce and remarriage. It was at this time that he began to communicate more often with his mother and father through letters. Still, they never completely understood. The incongruence between his parents' evaluation of his writing and the world's acclaim is highlighted by Hugh Walpole's comment: "We have no short story writer alive in England as good as the author of 'The Killers.' " However, as a twist, Walpole added, "but then neither has America," for Hemingway was residing in Europe at the time.

CHAPTER **6**

Ernest took his new bride, Pauline, to the quiet Southern town of Key West, Florida in 1928. Here, they found a subtropical island village blessed with clear blue skies, blue-green ocean, trade winds rustling through the stately palms, and a slow pace of life. Key West was a phenomenal discovery for Ernest; the atmosphere, the climate, and the culture immediately invigorated and stimulated him. Here, on this northernmost island of the Caribbean, he worked on *A Farewell to Arms*. Pauline soon became pregnant. Ernest found great fishing off the keys, particularly in the Marquesa Keys, some 25 miles away by boat. He caught kingfish, tarpon, barracudas, snappers, groupers, and various types of sharks, including man-eaters. He particularly enjoyed pitting himself against the big fish off Key West. For him, it was a perfect total environment for work and exhilarating physical experiences.

Hemingway felt an enormous identification with anything physical. He felt very close to all kinds of animals and especially liked cats, dogs, and birds (in many cases, more than humans, according to what he told friends.) In his book, *The Old Man and the Sea*, the old fisherman gives the small bird advice on taking rest on the boat and then going on with life, taking its chances just as man must do. Hemingway often questioned the physical weaknesses in life, which is brought out well when the old fisherman asks the bird why it is so tired, when, in fact, the night is windless and the flying should be easy. He wonders what is happening to the birds today, that they tire so easily on a night that is good for flying. The old man also identifies closely with the huge marlin he has caught on his line in terms of its exhaustion, a deep fatigue he has felt in the past and one which he knows the great fish is suffering as it pauses while struggling to free itself.

Hemingway frequently sought relief from complex interpersonal relationships by attempting to identify with the problems of wildlife. He talks about going beyond the people of the world when he is searching out the big fish in *The Old Man and the Sea.*

He also experienced some guilt in destroying wildlife, though he certainly was active in bringing death to innumerable wild creatures. He speaks of the sin of killing the beautiful fish in *The Old Man and the Sea,* then rationalizes the catch by reflecting on the old Indian adage, "One kills only what one eats." In this work he seems to be saying that he is a hunter and a fisherman, born to hunt and fish, and thus, that he need not to justify his activity. He also is saying that, if he were only a fisherman, he would not have to give any thought to whether he should fish for sport.

Ernest and Pauline relocated to Kansas City for a short period. Here, their first child, Patrick, was born. The three of them soon returned to the Florida Keys. Within a couple of years, they would travel to Kansas City again, for the birth of their second son. Ernest and Pauline had two sons in the first four years of their marriage. At this time, Ernest was elated over *A Farewell to Arms,* which he felt was the greatest book he had written.

In the late 1920s, Ernest's father grew ill and became increasingly weak. He was found to have diabetes mellitus, an inability to metabolize sugar properly. Some accounts state that he put off treatment. On learning that he had diabetes, he became increasingly distressed, and soon, there was a noticeable decline in his morale. His condition grew worse. Then, on December 6, 1928, in the privacy of his bedroom, Dr. Hemingway shot himself behind the ear, using his father's Smith and Wesson revolver.

Ernest was on a train trip between New York and Arkansas when he received the telegram advising him of his father's death. He came straight to Chicago and began to make arrangements for the funeral.

In the wake of the tragedy, Ernest provided enormous strength to the entire family. He gave advice and counsel to all. He helped his family to accept that, though Dr. Hemingway had been a deacon in the church and was admired by many, he had, in fact, committed the ultimate sin, suicide. This would be little understood, he led them to see, and probably would be held in contempt by many townspeople. Interestingly, according to the accounts, Ernest told his family that he wanted no crying at the funeral. Crying, he said, might do for other people, but not for the Hemingways. Ernest admired courage, and this was reflected in his psychological comforting of the family members. He emphasized his own values to them and projected his need to show not only his own strength, but that of every member of the

Hemingway family. Giving way to grief was not a Hemingway trait, in Ernest's mind.

Dr. Hemingway's suicide had a profound impact on Ernest's thinking, as might be expected. His father's death provided a behavior pattern for him which he also would adopt ultimately to escape his decreasing vitality and encroaching problems. It appeared to be a very manly way out of seemingly unbearable problems. Interestingly, not only did Ernest's father commit suicide, but the father of his first wife, Hadley, also died from a self-inflicted gunshot wound.

Also significant is that Ernest established a lifestyle of escapism very early. He ran whenever problems or people started moving in on him. Michigan, World War I, the Spanish Civil War, World War II, writing, safaris, Key West, the *Pilar,* romantic escapades, Havana, his divorces, Ketchum—all were avenues he took to preclude his being forced to "stand and fight." There are two intriguing and obvious aspects of Ernest Hemingway's escapism. First, he fabricated names for everyone. He even called himself "Dr. Hemingstein." (This became such a well-established name that his brother called him "Stein," even into later life.) All of the others in his circle of acquaintances took on the names Ernest assigned. Some may say this is a trait of his rich imaginativeness. While this may be true in part, his "re-naming" habit also subtly relates to the pattern of escapism he established early in life. A second facet of this escapism was his concern about his age. Ernest usually added a couple of years when referring to his age, and few of his friends knew his real age. The significance of this trait is evident when viewed in relation to his drive to escape his contemporary reality; yet, he rationalized this escapism too well to have ever recognized it consciously. His insistence on "standing up and taking it (whatever life threw his way) like a man," his stated credo, rings untrue at times in reviewing his actions from a less emotional, more objective vantage point.

After all the details of his father's funeral and burial had been dispatched, Ernest returned to Key West. Here, he purchased a Spanish-style house, at 907 Whitehead Street. Pauline and Ernest soon added an extension at the rear of the house. After Pauline had a swimming pool installed, the extension became a pool house with dressing rooms. According to accounts, Pauline had the pool built without Ernest's knowledge while he was on a trip to Spain. When he returned and learned the pool had cost more than they had paid for the house, he exploded in a verbal furor that resounded throughout small island community. But his rage soon subsided, and he returned to his writing. Upstairs, there was a workroom for Ernest that could be reached by a catwalk from the second-story balcony.

He was busy in those days completing *A Farewell to Arms*, taking great pleasure in his young son, and attending boxing matches in Key West. Ernest always enjoyed a good fight, whether a boxing match or a street fracas. Many local fighters were boxing in Key West in those days, and when fair amounts of money were bet on the outcomes of the contests, certain dishonest pugilists began to "throw" the fights. Ernest reacted with anger. He became a member of a sort of "boxing commission," comprised of self-appointed locals. He did what he could to make certain the bouts remained honest. According to a local Key West story, on one occasion, Ernest bounded into the ring and hauled to his feet a fallen fighter who was feigning a knockout.

Ernest dressed very informally in Key West and became known for his Basque fishing shirts and khaki pants. Though still slender in those days, his large size made him quite noticeable as he ambled through the streets. Residents of Key West later characterized him as their first "hippie." He perplexed the local citizenry, and particularly the more conservative souls of this small southernmost town, some of whom regarded him as a writer of "dirty books." Their bewilderment was understandable. Here was an internationally-known novelist, a war hero, someone they expected to be highly predictable, someone with ready access to the highest levels of society in this small island community. However, Ernest's behavior, demeanor, and dress were totally antithetical to their stereotypes of a "world-famous author." He dressed like a fisherman. He walked the streets in grubby shorts, going barefoot at a time before bare feet were in vogue. He drank to excess and associated with the more unsavory characters of the area. From the viewpoint of the more traditional and influential Key West citizens, Ernest was not at all what they expected him to be.

The noted author seemed oblivious to their comments. He was enjoying his life in Key West. He particularly enjoyed the bird life on the various islands in the area and spent many happy mornings fishing off the islands and the Keys. In 1929, he became interested in exploring new territory off the Cuban coast. It was during these days in Key West that he gained the reputation of being a suntanned, whiskey-drinking fisherman. It is certainly true that he enjoyed catching marlin, drinking whiskey and soda as well as beer, and broiling himself beneath the hot island sun. Yet Ernest always seemed to keep his drinking under good control. He drank great quantities of whiskey, enjoyed it thoroughly, and even recorded stories about his escapades while under the spell of alcohol.

Ernest and Pauline made every effort to take advantage of their flexible lifestyle through travel. Their penchant for domestic travel was reflected in their seasonal activities—winter in Key West, summer in Michigan (and later in Ketchum), big-game hunting in the western United States, and duck-hunting in Arkansas.

Ernest had a number of friends. He particularly enjoyed male friends whom he could treat as kid brothers. He greatly needed the admiration of others and found it very difficult to tolerate any kind of criticism he regarded as other than intellectual. He liked to be in the limelight constantly, to be showing others "how," and to be looked up to. He also had a remarkable nonchalance about money—and the need to earn it. During the early 1930s, he often had difficulty raising as much as $200.00 at any given time. Yet, in order to enjoy extended fishing trips off the coast of Cuba, some of which lasted as long as two months, he would turn down offers to write short magazine articles that easily could have provided him funds to meet his needs while he was awaiting word about the sales of his books. He readily spent money to pursue his pleasures, particularly for trips to Spain and Tanganyika, and hunting junkets in Abyssinia.

In 1933, Ernest went to Havana in a friend's boat to do some deep-sea fishing. When he found the fish were not running, he took a room at the Hotel Ambos Mundos in Havana and started to work on a novel and several short stories. He would get up at five o'clock in the morning and work until ten, or, on productive days, until noon. Thus, he combined an enjoyable period of writing and fishing. He kept daily records of the fish he caught, the types of equipment he used, and his experiences on the water. He also maintained a daily log of the amount of writing he had done.

In November, Ernest and Pauline went to Paris, where he saw his first copy of *Winner Take Nothing* as the shipment of books arrived for sales in France. This was the first time Ernest had seen the book set in type. He had corrected the proofs by telegram because he had been out of touch with his publisher for an extended time while on various travels and fishing trips. From France, Ernest and Pauline went on to the Tyrol, then to various parts of Africa, including Kenya, where Ernest did a great deal of hunting.

It was in Kenya that Ernest came down with dysentery which almost took his life. But it was while he was recuperating from it, and under the influence of quinine and emetine, that he conceived some of his most popular stories. His experiences on the Serengeti Plain had influenced him enormously. The crack of the rifle, the heat, the exercise, the totally physical environment had formed one of the most enjoyable experiences of his life. He had hunted elk and antelope, buffalo and lions.

After returning to Key West early in April, Ernest found that he had received $3,000.00 as an advance for his work. This money finally enabled him to buy the fishing cruiser that he had wanted for years. Now his dream had come true. His return also marked the start of another very productive period. He worked steadily on *The Green Hills of Africa* and *To Have and Have Not*. He enjoyed developing characters for *To Have and Have Not* from persons who lived in Key West and a few who lived in Cuba. He also was having great fun on his new boat, the *Pilar*, catching barracuda, amberjack, and groupers.

During this period, Ernest enjoyed talking with the local people, especially in Sloppy Joe's Bar. He often arrived at three in the afternoon and spent several hours exchanging stories of hunting and fishing. He was always quite a storyteller and enjoyed using exaggeration for effect.

He also spent considerable time in the sun and immensely enjoyed the sea air. He enjoyed drinking beer and could guzzle unbelievable quantities of it. His fishing experiences between Key West and Florida provided him much of the material for *The Old Man and the Sea*. One of his most exciting fishing adventures had been catching a huge sailfish. The fish, taken after a four-hour battle, weighed 119 pounds. Today it is on display at the Miami Rod and Reel Club.

Hemingway expressed over and over in his writings that he was intent on distinguishing the living from the nonliving. A man of great mental and physical vigor, he had the rare capacity to live life to its fullest. In "The Snows of Kilimanjaro," he stated that all of us must make our livelihood wherever our talent lies. Hemingway, through his writing and throughout his life, made his livelihood by selling vitality.

He continued to work in the mornings on his book, though still plagued by the amoebic dysentery he had contracted in Africa. He was required to take castor oil, which he often chased with scotch or brandy. Ernest never lost his love for Africa and always yearned to return there to hunt and to immerse himself in the raw physical environment. He had another characteristic that was part of him always: he would be greatly enamored of things for a while, then quickly tire of their attraction. He became bored with almost every good thing he had and was forced to vary his activities to maintain a productive life style. He maintained, however, that he loved to write, to make love, and to hunt and fish, and he continued to do so until late in life.

About this time, his old friend, Gertrude Stein, published a book which stung him deeply. He felt that it was a malicious work. It galled him that readers of her book got the impression that she had taught him how to write. While it was widely accepted that she had influenced his style, Hemingway rejected this. He could never share the credit for his writing with anyone. Jealously, he guarded the personal ownership of his writing style and ability. This is obvious and understandable after considering the psychological significance of his works. Hemingway's writings were an extension of his ego. His writings were, in fact, him. His entire being was wrapped up in them. If he admitted someone else shared in his writing ability or style, then he could no longer be sure of his own identity. A great deal of time had to go by, and a great deal of maturation and growth in security had to take place, before he could acknowledge that Gertrude Stein had, indeed, influenced his writing style.

Ernest had his share of disagreements with any number of people and was quick to say what he thought and stand up for what he believed. There is a story about a fight Hemingway had with Joseph Knapp, a wealthy young publisher, on the docks at Bimini. Knapp and Hemingway got into an argument when Knapp accused the novelist of not catching as many fish as he claimed he had caught. This, we can see, was interpreted by Hemingway as an attack on his adequacy. In his view, if he did not perform in these traditionally masculine endeavors at the level he had set for himself, he had no way, acceptable to him, to prove his worth. By questioning his bravery, or his hunting or fishing skill, one was attacking the basic psychological structure of Ernest Hemingway's personality. The result was that a sizeable fight ensued, witnessed by a number of onlookers, including the Bimini Beach Boys Band, who later wrote a song about the incident which was to be sung throughout the Bahamas. During the fight, Hemingway had two toenails broken off, but he felt he had won the brawl. Later, he worried considerably about Mr. Knapp and whether or not he had been hurt. Knapp, after all, was an influential national publisher whose holdings included *Collier's, Woman's Home Companion,* and *The American Magazine.*

In another incident, Hemingway got into a heated disagreement with poet Archie MacLeish, who had come down to Key West to do some fishing with him. They were close friends—in fact, so close that one of Hemingway's first books was dedicated to Archibald MacLeish. The two of them were out on Hemingway's boat with no crew. They had fished together many times, but, on this day, they got into a heated conversation. They decided to continue the discussion on one of the nearby islands, where the poet disembarked. As MacLeish waited for his host to get off the boat, Hemingway simply turned the boat around and headed toward Key West, leaving MacLeish to spend a furious, solitary night on the small, uninhabited key. Ernest returned to pick up MacLeish the next day, but the two men never felt the same about one another again.

These two instances describe a type of behavior that characterized many of Ernest Hemingway's interpersonal relations. His precipitous manner of doing things was enigmatic to many, and especially to those who were close to him. Hemingway's behavior was not really inexplicable: in fact, one aspect of personality theory, dealing with the amount of control an individual exerts over his thoughts and actions, is useful in explaining much of his behavior. It is a much more useful explanation than that given by many of his friends—that Ernest had a quick temper which flared up with little or no provocation, or that Ernest was simply a self-made and self-proclaimed son-of-a-bitch. The psychological model to which we refer may be exemplified by a continuum of behavior. At one end of this continuum is high cortical control; at the opposite end is impulsivity. An individual who demonstrates, through personality characteristics, high cortical control is one who is concerned about the effects of his actions on the behavior of other people, as well as the values of other people and their interpretations of his actions. Such a person exhibits logical and highly controlled behavior. He rules out a great deal of emotionality in life and, as a result, stifles practically all spur-of-the-moment or impulsive behavior. He appears to be colorless, unoriginal, and rigid, as well as one who does not live life as freely and as enjoyably as others. The ideal personality, on this particular variable, would be an individual who does exert *some* cortical control but is able to relax this control in favor of what might be regarded as a benign control. Such a personality rationally yields to *some* impulsivity, yet does not become totally impulse-oriented.

At the opposite end of the continuum is impulsivity—or the total lack of cortical control. An individual at this end of the continuum is totally id-oriented and totally dominated by the basic impulses. He speaks without evaluating, acts without thinking, and is driven only by his feelings and not by his logic. He cares little, if at all, about the impact of his actions on others so long as these actions fulfill the needs he sees himself as having, or so long as they protect him from the psychological and physical onslaught of others. This causes him to "run over" friends and to be an irresponsible and, at times, unfeeling person. Ernest Hemingway, from all accounts, seems to have been essentially this latter type of personality. Though, at times, he was very attentive, concerned, sympathetic, and interested in people, he could, at the slightest provocation, react immediately in the opposite manner. He would flare up, strike out, and do what he "wanted" to do. It was as if he were driven to satisfy his needs without regard for the consequences of the manner in which he satisfied these needs. This type of behavior was most evident when he felt he had to prove himself, or to muster a psychological defense against an attack on his ego.

Ernest never thought of himself as handicapped in any way; yet he once had a revealing experience in this regard on arriving at Seney, on the upper peninsula of Michigan. He was recuperating at the time from injuries incurred while covering the Spanish Civil War, and, on getting off the train at Seney, Ernest heard the brakeman tell the engineer something to the effect that "There is a crippled person here who needs more time to get his bags down." Ernest was shocked, and, as the story goes, when he heard that, he stopped being a cripple, at least in his own mind. On this vacation, which was to allow him to recuperate, he got a number of ideas for "Big Two-hearted River"—the story of Nick Adams, who had gone on a hiking and fishing trip while recuperating from his war wounds.

Ernest had been baptized as a Catholic in 1918. Nine years later, in 1927, he made a real effort to get back into the good graces of his adopted Catholic heritage. Pauline was Catholic, and their wedding was set for the tenth of May in Paris, in a Catholic rite. Ernest told Catholic officials that Hadley had been a nonbeliever, and for this reason, their marriage, which had been performed in a Protestant church, was invalid. By this logic Hadley had never been his wife. Ernest also told the Church hierarchy that he had been baptized nine years earlier in Italy by a priest while he lay wounded amid rows of wounded men.

After they were married, in the summer of 1927, Ernest took Pauline to Spain and did many of the things that he and Hadley had done there before. Spain was much the same, and Ernest had a new wife. Pauline had to give him a good deal of freedom because Ernest needed to be "to himself." He did a considerable amount of writing during this time and finished "Ten Indians" and "Hills like White Elephants."

Hemingway's books were selling well, especially *The Sun Also Rises*, which had sold 23,000 copies by the fall of 1927. Literary critics were faulting his works, however, for overemphasizing vulgar people and their "sordid little affairs." He was "self-consciously virile," they said, from the standpoint of being obsessed in his writings with gunmen, mercenary soldiers, bullfighters, prostitutes, hard-drinkers; and dope fiends. Hemingway read many of the reviews and indicated that the criticisms made him self-conscious and discomfited. For this reason, he said, he had stopped reading them, and his work went on.

In December of 1928, while staying with Ernest, Bumby accidentally thrust his finger into his father's right eye. The cut was small, but it seriously injured the pupil in Ernest's good eye. As a result, his vision was sharply reduced. Later, he wrote to James Joyce (who himself was nearly blind), expressing concern about his fear of blindness. Ernest had an enormous fear of any kind of physical incapacity. Much of his activity was centered around proving that he possessed a full and superior physical endowment. His reaction to this "close call" lasted for an inordinate period, offering significant evidence of his disproportionate and irrational dread of blindness. The fact that he wrote to James Joyce at all revealed the depth of his fear and anxiety concerning blindness and, indeed, any physical disability.

Long before his airplane crashes in Africa, Ernest denied he was particularly accident-prone. He became frustrated with friends who chided him about the many accidents he seemed to suffer and, more maddeningly, that some of these mishaps had been caused by a certain physical clumsiness. One such incident occurred late one night, in 1928, when he inadvertently tugged a skylight cord hanging in the bathroom. The skylight crashed down upon him, cutting him deeply above his right eye. Shaken by this, Ernest began to feel clumsy, awkward, and rather ridiculous. He was threatened by this mishap because it did not square with his self-concept of the indomitable man who overcomes all obstacles. He began to ruminate to some of his friends concerning his problems with stomach sickness, infection, the cut in his eye made by Bumby's fingernail, and the humiliating skylight debacle.

Though these experiences were traumatic for Hemingway, he did not shrink from examining them, for his task as a novelist was to find the life-meaning in all that happened to him. He had to seize, dissect, examine, and stroke until the essence revealed any attractive or intriguing possibilities out there—for himself, or for someone else. This dissection led to an understanding of the beautiful and the ugly parts of the life experiences available to most of us—if we are free to do our own seizing, holding to ourselves objects of mystery and appeal. Hemingway's unique talent lay in being able to communicate feelings, experiences, motives noble or base, and the inner workings of so many things which both attract and repel the more reasonable—or, should we say, the more timid or fearful—among us.

If we shrink from seizing and exploiting what we want from out there, we must turn for the understanding of life's essences to one who does not avoid the adventure and its risk. Fear of consequences seems to be one of many arresting, stultifying, and immobilizing ways the superego uses to keep us at arm's length from some of life's sweetest rewards—all in the service of our presumed safety and security. But safe people aren't much fun, and what is security when everybody is going to die anyway? So—we superego-oriented need our id-oriented, especially those who can communicate experiences and their inner meaning; or, how are we to know of life? Hemingway's talent, his craft, are gifts not only to the bold, but particularly to the faint, gifts that transcend the human fallibility of their bestower. Through his work, for as long as mankind reads, he has attained a stature, an immortality deserved by few.

Some superego-oriented personalities produce books and leave them behind, but many of these messages are proscriptions *against* feeling and experiencing rather than prescriptions *for* tasting the flavor of life, for better or worse. Hemingway's legacy adds zest for the self-actualized and the adventurous among us; but particularly for those of us who are more constricted, his work can be one of the few handles we will ever have on the realities of experience or the keys to deeper feeling. So, who needs the id-driven? We all do. And we consume them every bit as much as they consume everything in sight, including, at the end, their own selves. On the dark side, some id-driven leave behind only a wake of exploited lives. The remarkable among them may leave behind art and understanding. By that definition, Hemingway has been among the most remarkable of all. So many writers give us ideas and try to tell us what we should feel. Hemingway gave us feelings, and never tried to tell us what our ideas about them should be.

CHAPTER 7

It was in December of 1936 that Ernest first met Martha Gellhorn. He was sitting in Sloppy Joe's Bar in Key West, having a drink and talking with local friends when several tourists came in. They were sightseeing around Key West while on vacation from their home in St. Louis. Martha, called "Marty," was with her mother, who was in her mid-fifties, and her younger brother, Alfred.

The story is that Hemingway was dressed in shorts and looked dirty and rather rough. Nevertheless, he introduced himself to them and spoke of his familiarity with St. Louis. Martha had attended Bryn Mawr, had written a novel, *What Mad Pursuit*, and also had published a collection of short stories titled *The Trouble I've Seen*.

The visitors were fascinated by Ernest, who radiated charm and cordiality. He showed them around the Key West area and introduced them to Pauline. Mrs. Gellhorn and Alfred soon left Key West, but Martha stayed on for a while. She very much enjoyed being squired about by Ernest Hemingway. All of this, of course, gave rise to more tongue-clucking among the local people. Yet, even though Martha was a significant diversion in his life, Ernest continued to write, especially in the mornings.

He was to see her again at the Gran Via Hotel in Valencia while covering the Spanish Civil War in 1937. By this time, Ernest was calling her "daughter," and they spent time together as he showed her the Spanish terrain and the activities of the troops as they prepared for the anticipated attacks.

Hemingway really found great joy again in covering the war in Spain. He loved adversity, exulted in being part of it, and, if not part of it, at least being near it. He had written, in *The Green Hills of Africa*, about the brotherhood of soldiers and their dependence on one another. He loved Spain and the Spanish people. He identified with them and wished them success.

At the same time, Hemingway felt that to seek adventures

was to blunt the instrument of his livelihood. He believed that extensive traveling, or exciting, strenuous, or stimulating activity pulls an author away from the daily discipline of writing. Then, it takes even greater diligence, if not sheer agony, to settle back to writing. Yet, he deemed the adventures and experiences essential if an author is to have something of major importance to say. He felt that many potentially good writers have nothing significant to communicate because of a dearth of meaningful personal experiences. He expressed this view in the preface to the *Short Stories of Ernest Hemingway,* published by Scribner's.

Just before he left Spain in 1937, after completing work on the film *The Spanish Earth,* Hemingway was given a farewell party on May Day by the Twelfth Brigade. On his return to the United States, he went to Key West. There, he made plans to spend some time during that summer on the island of Bimini, relaxing and writing.

On June 2nd of that year, Hemingway received a telegram indicating that the President and Mrs. Roosevelt wished to see the film, *The Spanish Earth,* and would be pleased to have his company at the screening in the White House. The interest on the part of the Roosevelts apparently had been sparked by Miss Gellhorn, who was a friend of the First Lady. This greatly impressed Ernest, who was not immune to the aura enjoyed by the well-placed, and the spin-off in personal fame from spending an evening with the Roosevelts. Ernest accepted the invitation. Apparently, he liked Eleanor, whom he found charming, but disliked the President, whom he regarded as somewhat effeminate. Ernest associated paralysis with lack of physical vigor, which, in turn, he equated with a lack of masculinity. That, coupled with his general dislike for politicians (most of whom he thought held power through false pretenses), dampened his enjoyment of the occasion.

Throughout his life, Hemingway kept in touch with current events, but he was an anti-intellectual with little respect for those who had achieved on a higher plane than he felt he had. This is supported by Seward's statement in his book, *My Friend Hemingway,* indicating he was the only university professor Ernest Hemingway liked. As to politics, Hemingway felt that, for the most part, it was a false art, one which employed frequent deception and gave power to those who really had not proven their ability to handle it. In reality, this verbalized disdain may well have been a manifestation of his own envy. Such grudging usually is a disquieting signal from our innermost fears of personal inadequacy.

Soon after the White House screening, Ernest received the

galley proofs of *To Have and Have Not*. Ernest worked them over. When he finished them, he decided to return to Spain. He led his relatives and friends to believe that this was a matter of some considerable personal sacrifice. However, he could hardly wait to return to Spain and the war. During this period, he was doing extremely well, emotionally. His writing was being favorably received, and he was riding a crest of self-confidence.

This also was one of the periods in which Hemingway felt particularly free from anxiety. For a major portion of his life, he had been visited by anxiety. Later, it became an almost constant companion. Anxiety is a feeling all of us experience, to varying degrees. It is a personality factor that helps us mobilize our physical and psychic resources to combat a threat, be it an external *objective* threat or an internal *neurotic* one. While the cause of the anxiety may vary, the reaction does not.

The anxiety which results from an identifiable *objective* threat is much more psychologically adaptive than that which originates from neurosis. This more adaptive type of apprehensiveness is called "fear." The psychologically maladaptive type of anxiety which Ernest Hemingway experienced in some measure throughout his life, and more intensely during his later years, is often called "free-floating" anxiety. This is because it has no clear-cut or objective reference point. The individual is anxiety-ridden, but he cannot tell why since he has no clear understanding of the source of the threat. He just feels threatened and suffers countless vague but pervasive emotional consequences.

"Free-floating" anxiety, out of control, can be totally debilitating. It not only interferes with the thought processes, but has a major impact on bodily function. The individual experiencing "free-floating" anxiety usually complains of a racing heart, palpitations, even dizziness. He is grouchy and easily irritated by the behavior of others. He frequently complains of generalized weakness or faintness, such as pains in the chest, headaches, trembling, insomnia, and shortness of breath or other difficulty in breathing. He also exhibits a lowered frustration tolerance. At the slightest thwarting of his desires or interference with his imagined rights in his own domain, he becomes frustrated—even enraged. This rage, externalized or directed inward, is often regarded as having been brought about by an "anxiety attack."

Since an anxiety attack exerts such widespread impact on the individual's physical condition, he becomes overly sensitive to the physiological functions of his body. In other words, he frequently becomes, to varying degrees, hypochondriacal. Physiological processes of the body to which he was previously unconscious now become focal points of concern. This type of thought pattern reduces a person's creative effectiveness. He feels menaced but, unable to identify the source of the threat, he remains mobilized, on guard, to defend against it. This constant mobilization precludes his thinking of anything other than being prepared for impending doom. He is tense and excitable; noise or confusion are totally intolerable to him. He may well become apathetic and experience a loss of appetite (both for food and sex). If he indulges in either eating or sex, the activity may seem meaningless. Both eating and sex may take on a barren, even automaton-like, reflex quality.

At times, when Hemingway was caught up in an anxiety reaction, he gleaned insights that disordered thought patterns were interfering with his productivity. It is an accepted premise, in psychology, that involved and long-standing anxiety reactions can inhibit productivity and cripple creativity.

Because of his lack of writing output during seiges of anxiety, Hemingway became severely depressed. He felt worthless, inadequate, and inferior. From early adulthood, his feelings of adequacy had centered almost entirely on his writing ability. Hemingway had no other dependable source of ego identification or ego gratification than developing and exhibiting his craft. He derived some ego satisfaction from projecting a forced image of maleness through his adventurous exploits (sex, hunting, fishing, and a capacity to imbibe large amounts of alcohol), but his primary source of identity was his writing. So long as he could write, he had visible proof that he was an adequate individual. And so long as he could write successfully, he could prove that his parents' disapproval of his chosen vocation was unfounded.

When his creativity failed, however, even though perhaps temporarily, he lost this buffer between the reality of his parents' rejection of his profession and his concept of his own ability. It is interesting to note that Ernest Hemingway, intermittently throughout his life, felt he had lost his ability to write, or was on the verge of losing it—forever. He was always on guard against this eventuality. To prevent having his ability to write escape from him overnight, he employed what appears to be a simplistic stratagem: he never finished a day's writing with a complete thought. Instead, he always left an unfinished idea to begin with the next day. This reflects his fear of the transitory nature of his writing talent, a fear which he carried with him throughout his life.

When his creativity was supplanted by anxiety, Hemingway became fully resigned to the final eclipse of his talent. He felt, at the end, that his creative well had gone dry irrevocably—after so many years of dreading that very disaster. We believe that, if he could have realized his writing skill had been only temporarily supplanted by anxiety and had not truly deserted him, his major motivation for suicide would have been removed. In fact, his "loss" was a self-fulfilling prophecy. He had made the prediction early in life and, later, it was fulfilled: his writing skills abandoned him. If, as he perceived, his skills were gone, then there was little else to sustain him. The very basis of his feelings of adequacy, maleness, and importance was gone.

It is easier to understand the emotional impact of his various disabilities and illnesses and the threat of the loss of writing ability when one understands the relationship between the illness, or these seeming deficits, and his view of the purpose of his body. A person's view of the purpose of his body may be illustrated by the use of a continuum. At one end of the continuum is the "tool" concept; at the opposite end is the "esthetic-stimulus" concept. A person who adopts the tool concept views his body as a tool to accomplish work. He measures his adequacy in terms of the effectiveness of his body in being productive. This work may be either physical, as in the case of a laborer, or creative, as in the case of a writer such as Hemingway, or an artist or composer. Or this work may be intellectual, like that performed by theoreticians or academicians. However, the one common thread that all of these people possess is a *single criterion* for adequacy. That criterion is the effectiveness or productivity of the "tool"—their body.

In contrast, people who adopt the "esthetic-stimulus" concept are concerned with the *stimulus* value of the body. They believe that the body should bring pleasure to others when they look at it. In this view of the purpose of the body, there is no implication of the need for productivity—only the need for providing pleasure to others who behold the body. With this concept, the body goes beyond just its physical configuration, smoothness of skin, hair, and coloration, and includes the mind; therefore, actors, dancers, poets, and singers—from opera stars to pop performers—singers—are apt to lean toward the esthetic-stimulus concept of body purpose.

Historically, cultures have tended to gravitate toward one end of this continuum or the other. For example, ancient peoples in the Greek city-state of Athens tended toward the esthetic-stimulus concept in viewing their bodies. As a result, the citizens of Athens did not work. Work and other purely productive activities were relegated to slaves. While the Athenians did study to improve their minds, it was not as a concentrated *productive* activity, *per se*. Learning was a deliberate effort to become more attractive and acceptable, as well better equipped to understand the complexities of the world. A major preoccupation of these people was the improvement of the body and the mind.

In contrast, the ancient Romans were a militaristic people whose adequacy was measured in terms of the productivity of the individual, and of the culture. As a result, more "things" were bequeathed to us by the Romans than by the Greeks. While the Greeks left an esthetic heritage of art, literature, and scholasticism, the Romans' heritage endowed more practical ideas—about aqueducts, roads, and public health systems.

The American culture today tends toward the middle of the continuum. We pride ourselves on being a highly productive people—strongly tool-oriented—yet we are also deeply concerned with the esthetic-stimulus value of our bodies. This is reflected in the size of our billion-dollar cosmetics industry, men's as well as women's.

Returning to our original statement, in order to better understand the emotional impact of Hemingway's various illnesses and of the threat of losing his writing skill or productivity, we must understand the relationship between these deficiencies, real or threatened, and his view of the purpose of his body. If a person who views his body primarily as a "tool" suffers an illness or disability that mars his appearance, the psychological impact of this will be minimal—or, at least, much less than the psychological impact of a condition that substantially reduces his productivity. Conversely, a person subscribing to the esthetic-stimulus concept who suffers a disability or illness that substantially detracts from his appearance will experience a greater psychological impact than if the disabling condition merely reduces his productivity or the *tool* value of his body.

As in all continua in psychology, no person is totally at one extreme or the other. While individuals tend toward one end, no one ever reaches the extreme. In other words, no one is totally "tool" oriented or totally "esthetic-stimulus" oriented. Human behavior, and the antecedents to human behavior, are too complex to permit rigid labeling by such a simplistic device as finding segments of the population clustered at either pole or continuum end-point; however, it helps in understanding complex behavior to estimate where individuals fall in relation to given end-points.

Ernest Hemingway, for example, tended toward the tool end-point, being, from all evidence, almost totally tool-oriented. He gained his feelings of accomplishment from his productivity, from the effectiveness of his body and mind. When he was attractive, charming and well-received, but also nonproductive, his behavior would become morose, and he would sink into the depths of depression—consumed with self-doubts. Conversely, he could be rejected by others, even such significant others as his wife and family, but if at that time he was productive, he would be ecstatic and ebullient. During such times, he even could gloss over the rejection of others by agreeing with them that he was, in fact, an s.o.b., and then promptly forget it. Productivity was one of the keys to his mood swings. There are many other indications that Hemingway was a tool-oriented person. These include his neglect, at times, of personal hygiene, his careless personal appearance and sloppy dress, his concern about his vision, his rigid goals for the number of pages of manuscript to be written daily, and his meticulous recording of the fish he caught and the types of equipment he used. But the key indication is the ease with which his "free-floating" anxiety was precipitated by his fear of the loss of productivity.

At the height of his success and self-confidence, Hemingway still had difficulties in coping with adverse criticism. One famous story concerns an episode in 1937 when Hemingway met Max Eastman in the office of a mutual friend. Eastman had written a widely-read review of Hemingway's *Death in the Afternoon* which he had titled "Bull in the Afternoon." Hemingway felt that the review was a derogatory personal assault. He accused Eastman of saying in the review that he (Hemingway) was impotent. Eastman denied it. A short scuffle ensued. Afterward, Eastman claimed to have beaten Hemingway fairly in a wrestling match. Hemingway later told reporters that this had been braggadocio on Eastman's part and that it had not happened that way at all. The point to be made is that, even at the height of his success, Hemingway could be emotionally unsettled by negative reviews of his work. When reporters later asked him about the episode, he issued a strident, if baseless, challenge to Eastman, who wasn't present at the time. This incident demonstrates that Hemingway was almost totally "tool"-oriented. The deepest cut of all from Hemingway's point of view was a critical swipe at his productivity. He was sensitive about his writing skills, and even more sensitive about the effectiveness of his body and its productivity in terms of "maleness," such as matters of virility, bravery, hunting and fishing knowledge and skill, and athletic prowess. If one attacked Hemingway on any of these fronts, the lines of battle loomed up almost immediately. Yet he was almost completely impervious to comments that denigrated his appearance or the esthetic-stimulus value of his body.

On returning to Spain to cover the civil war, Ernest spent a good deal of time with Martha Gellhorn. He was impressed by how well she endured the rough going of a foreign correspondent covering a war. He considered her a courageous, tough, and hardy girl, and admired her greatly.

On one occasion, in October, 1937, Martha and Ernest were

CHAPTER 7

nearly killed when rebel artillerymen spotted the Ford they were driving and thought it belonged to the enemy. Shells and projectiles were fired at them but, luckily, they were not hit. This shared crisis seemed to increase the emotional depths of their relationship and drew them even closer.

Hemingway was covering the war in Spain when *To Have and Have Not* reached the market. Again there were negative reviews by critics, and Hemingway reacted angrily. He never forgot the reviewers who made critical comments about the book.

During this time, he was writing a play, which was to be produced as *The Fifth Column*. The character Philip Rawlings in the play was actually Hemingway's projection of himself. Rawlings was a correspondent who was secretly serving as a counterspy in Madrid during the Spanish Civil War. The character of Dorothy Bridges is thought to have been based on Martha Gellhorn. In this work, Ernest was obliquely cruel to his wife, Pauline, as he described in a thinly-veiled fashion what he liked about "Dorothy Bridges." This was a continuation of his growing rejection of Pauline, which first came to notice in *The Snows of Kilimanjaro*. He even went so far, in *The Fifth Column,* as to describe places he would like to visit with "Dorothy." These were the same places to which he had already taken Pauline in Cuba, France, and Kenya.

Less than one year after Ernest had left a seemingly happy existence in Key West, he was so involved with Martha and the civil war in Spain that he could hardly envision resuming his former life in Key West. However, he did return and soon was consumed by a compulsion to write stories about his experiences, especially those in Madrid. He was deeply troubled by feelings of guilt growing out of his disloyalty to Pauline. He was dealing again with many of the same emotions that had plagued him when he had left Hadley. He became irritable and overreactive to whatever was said, either in praise or rebuke, by friends or by those he disliked.

Hemingway tried to "work off" his hostility in physical activities, including refereeing boxing matches in Key West. But, in March, 1938, he boarded the *Ile de France* for Europe and then to Spain. During this sojourn, his writings echoed particular humanity and compassion toward the Spanish refugees. He had an enormous capacity for humanism, and this was evinced in his account of an episode that occurred on a trip to the Ebro Delta. As he and a traveling companion looked on, a truck loaded with Spanish loyalist soldiers turned over in a ditch. Many of the passengers were killed or injured. Hemingway raced forward to help them. He worked long and hard attempting to bring the survivors treatment, help, and comfort. His fellow traveler, Joe North, never forgot Hemingway's efforts in behalf of the throngs of unfortunate soldiers.

During this interval, Hemingway was covering the war in Spain for the North American Newspaper Alliance (NANA). His employers became somewhat disenchanted with his articles, indicating he seemed to be bent on shocking the readers by repeatedly discussing the grim details of battle, such as blown-off arms or legs and seeming to revel in these blood-and-guts accounts. His reports had a boastful tone, implying he was alone during many of these adventures at the front, when, in fact, he had several people with him—including Martha Gellhorn, on many occasions. He also gave his readers the impression that he was always near the line of fire and almost constantly in danger.

It was characteristic of Ernest that, by late August, 1938, he would dedicate *The Fifth Column* "to Marty (and a friend, Herbert) with love"—Marty, of course, being Martha Gellhorn. This was at a time when Pauline had agreed to accompany him to Wyoming so they could escape the summer heat of Key West. The dedication was a rather blatant public acknowledgment of what already was known in Barcelona, Paris, Madrid, and New York—Ernest's relationship with Martha. For some reason, this dedication did not appear in the book when it was published.

By February, 1939, Ernest had returned to Cuba. There, he established a pattern of working from approximately 7:30 in the morning until one or two in the afternoon, then satisfying his craving for physical exertion by engaging in fishing, tennis, or swimming. He finished a new story about the Spanish Civil War titled "Under the Ridge," the setting for which was a hilltop where the Twelfth International Brigade had just launched an unsuccessful attack. Its protagonist was a man named Badajoz, who was rebelling against the tactics of the military police. A perpetual rebel himself, against numerous social and political institutions, Ernest expressed his restiveness through many such characterizations.

In March, Ernest returned to Key West to see Bumby. He was unable to do much meaningful writing there because Pauline had many friends coming by constantly. Thus, in April, he left for Havana, hoping to be able to write an important novel there, as well as to indulge in the abundant outdoor activity he enjoyed. Soon Martha Gellhorn joined him there. She located an old house, called *Finca Vigia*, some 15 miles from Havana in the village of San Francisco de Paula.

Ernest did not like the house on learning that it was in a state of disrepair. He had never liked physical labor and considered it a

CHAPTER 7

waste of his time to engage in menial tasks such as yard work or painting. Martha, however, did considerable work on the house. After seeing it, Ernest decided liked it after all and moved in. However, he maintained a separate mailing address so it would not be known that he and Martha were living together. Here, Ernest resumed working productively, writing approximately 500 to 1,200 words a day. He also limited his alcohol intake to about three scotches before dinner.

Ernest was always concerned about the welfare of his children. Thus, he was deeply upset to learn in the summer of 1939 that a polio epidemic was raging in Key West. Pauline was with friends in Europe at the time and had left their two sons, Patrick and Gregory, in Key West. Ernest immediately sent money to a friend in Key West, J. B. Sullivan, and told him to send their two sons to New York, where he hoped they would be out of harm's way.

In the years since their divorce, Ernest had maintained a good relationship with Hadley and had kept in touch with her by letters even after her remarriage. Once, in July of 1939, when Hadley and her husband returned home from a fishing trip, they found Ernest's car parked near theirs. He was listening to the radio and waiting for them to return home. They reacted with surprise: they had not seen Ernest for approximately 10 years. Nonetheless, they had a cordial reunion, with the conversation centering chiefly on Bumby. Ernest enjoyed their exchange. He believed that Hadley was one of the finest persons he had ever known. He had great admiration for his first wife and a real need to continue on a warm, friendly basis with her. He seemed to assuage his conscience by assuring himself that she was doing well.

It is interesting not only that he kept in touch with Hadley, but that, when his marriage to Pauline began to founder in 1939, he informed Hadley that he felt Pauline's conduct had been inappropriate and poor. He related an incident in which he had told Pauline he wanted to visit with her and their two sons in Key West. Pauline, he said, had replied that, if he were coming just to get away from Cuba for a while, it would be best if he did not come.

When they decided to separate, Ernest wrote to Pauline's parents. He plaintively allowed that his work on his book had required a great deal of time away and that he had been very lonely. He also assured them that he would continue to look after her material needs and those of the boys.

CHAPTER 8

In 1940, Ernest was adjusting relatively well to life's various demands and was working hard on *For Whom the Bell Tolls*. He continued to write from early in the morning until early afternoon, having a drink or two before lunch, then playing tennis and fishing. Often, after the afternoons' physical activities, there were drinking sessions and conversations with the various interesting people he was meeting in Havana. He began to indulge in episodes of heavy drinking at least once a week in the *Floridita*, a cantina in Havana. On these occasions, he stayed out until the early hours of the morning and later told friends that drinking was necessary to counteract the exhausting work of writing. After these drinking excesses, he often was unable to work due to the terrible hangovers that frequently lasted late into the morning. This drinking not only led to diminished physical and creative ability, but it eventually culminated in cirrhosis of the liver. It is an interesting paradox that Ernest Hemingway was so concerned with the effectiveness of his body, yet worked assiduously to violate it.

By May of 1940, Ernest was complaining to friends that his wife, Pauline, was giving him a hard time. She was talking about him, he said, and it was bothering him. He indicated that she did not like the idea that he could write a good book while living with someone other than her. At the same time, he was particularly distressed to lose her objective and critical appraisal of his work, because he felt Pauline was one of those knowledgeable people who could discern the true value of writing. Also aggravating him was that his mother continued to urge him to attempt to create "constructive" literature.

At this time, Martha was becoming more and more vexed about the poor political administration of the countries she loved: the United States, Spain, and certain other European nations. She had political awareness, relatively unique among women in those pre-liberation days, of problems emanating from the wasting of government funds, increased taxation, and other hardships imposed on the people.

In contrast, Ernest was heavily and self-centeredly absorbed in his work. He had little patience for discussing Martha's needs or concerns, and he would not take the time to relate to her. This led to increasing disagreements until she left in a bit of a huff to spend a month in New York. He could be grossly selfish and thoughtless, as was evidenced on Martha's return, when he was to meet her at the train station at 2 p.m. She was bringing her mother with her, she had informed him. Ernest was at a bar, where he had fallen into a conversation about one of his books. He failed even to have Martha paged and notified that he would not meet her. Martha was furious. Later, she vehemently upbraided him for his selfishness and his rude indifference to her return.

For Whom the Bell Tolls was a novel in which Ernest took great pride. He felt that the writing was tight and good, knew he had worked awfully hard on it, and admitted it had cost him one wife in the process. Martha and Ernest had been living together now for three years and were making plans to be married once his divorce from Pauline was final.

The book *For Whom the Bell Tolls* was dedicated to Martha Gellhorn. As Ernest's friends were helping him read the proofs, they realized from the unfolding story that his father must have shot himself. Ernest told them that this was true. He went on to say that suicide was a common-sense way for many people to end their lives when they should be ended. He believed suicide was both practical and permissible when the going got too rough. It was during this rumination that he described to Martha a unique method of suicide by shotgun: one could discharge full blast through the barrel, he said, by placing one's toe on the trigger and bearing down.

Agility with a shotgun was also the focal point of Hemingway's first meeting with Gary Cooper while in Sun Valley in 1940. Cooper played Robert Jordan in the motion picture *For Whom the Bell Tolls*. Hemingway liked Cooper, but was stunned to discover that the actor was an excellent rifle shot—better, in fact, than Hemingway, who immediately "covered" his shooting performance by saying that he had drunk too much for too many years. He reacted by chiding Cooper about his smart clothes, as well as by kidding him about his "short" ability with a shotgun.

Whenever Ernest had an opportunity to be outdoors, as was the case when he took Martha on a tracking trip for a week or so into the middle-fork region of the Salmon River, he felt revitalized and somewhat restored. He also drank less, and this, according to the people closest to him, was a sign that he was getting a good hold on himself again and was more stable and in control of his emotions.

The new book, *For Whom the Bell Tolls,* initially received generally good reviews. Hemingway was pleased with most of them. He continued to bristle at any kind of adverse criticism and often attempted to respond to friends, defending his work against such comments. The film studios were interested in buying motion-picture rights to the work, and Hemingway experienced a substantial upswing in mood.

On November 4, 1940, he learned that his divorce from Pauline was final. He was charged with desertion, and she was awarded custody of their two sons. They had been married 13 years. During that time, Ernest had written seven books. He also had greatly enjoyed frequent trips to Europe and had been on an African safari and other memorable outings in Montana and Wyoming. His home in Key West and his fishing trips on the *Pilar* had brought him much pleasure. Interestingly, he did not accept as much of the blame for the termination of this marriage as he had for the end of his union with Hadley. He verbalized that the breakup had largely resulted from poor sexual adjustment, which soon gave rise to all sorts of murky speculation that Pauline, a devout Catholic who could bear no more children, was not completely stable. Ernest and Martha were married in Cheyenne, Wyoming on November 20, 1940.

Even though he and Martha had been living together for four years, Ernest seemed to find a good deal of relief in "being legal." While his id orientation provided him considerable freedom from guilt feelings in many areas in which he was beyond the bounds of societal mores and the morals prescribed by the Church, the idea of being married seemed to comfort Ernest enormously. It also closed one more avenue to criticism of his personal behavior.

CHAPTER 9

Soon after their marriage, Martha accepted an assignment from *Collier's* to cover the war in China. She and Ernest made plans to go to Hong Kong.

For Whom the Bell Tolls was beginning to receive poor reviews. Generally, the book was said to be a distorted if not slanderous view of the war in Spain. Critics accused Hemingway of not truly understanding the relevance of the Spanish war in relation to what was going on in the rest of the world in 1940, especially with regard to Fascism and its spreading influence. Many said that Hemingway simply did not have the depth of understanding needed to depict in writing the political nuances of the bloody Spanish overture to the global nightmare that was now unfolding. Still others said that, in *For Whom the Bell Tolls,* Hemingway had done what Fredrick Henry had done: he had deserted Spain when democracy succumbed. All of these criticisms disturbed Ernest enormously, especially when they came from people he knew well and respected.

On their way to the Far East, Ernest and Martha stopped in Hawaii. He had agreed to meet with some professors from the University of Hawaii to discuss his books. Disturbed by the unfriendly response of critics to *For Whom the Bell Tolls,* he was uncomfortable during the presentation. In the grip of a rather normal type of anxiety reaction, he particularly felt the need for some wine and asked for it. After several glasses, he became more relaxed. But, at one point, he had trouble pronouncing the word "periphery." Hemingway was deeply embarrassed. He tried to cover his slip of the tongue by pretending to be somewhat illiterate. He continued to degrade himself and at one point even recommended that the professors not assign their students to read *For Whom the Bell Tolls* because it was an immoral book. Obviously, he did not enjoy his ego-destructive encounter with the university professors, despite their efforts to be supportive. That

Hemingway saw the affair as intimidating, leading to a debacle of his own making, is revealing of his sensitivity to criticism, whether or not it was even in the offing.

Soon thereafter, Hemingway was a guest at a Hawaiian luau. After drinking quite a bit, and answering a number of questions posed by a freelance writer named Bishop, most of which made Hemingway uneasy and defensive, he challenged Bishop to a fist-fight. The fight did not ensue, however; Bishop excused himself and departed. Ernest's ego seems to have been salved by Bishop's exit. Once again, he had escaped by calling on physical violence as a means of avoiding critical confrontation and the feelings of inadequacy it aroused in him.

Ernest and Martha arrived in Hong Kong. They checked into the Repulse Bay Hotel. Ernest liked China; he liked the vibrations, the "lay of the land," and found the people to be frank and intelligent.

One interesting incident occurred in Hong Kong that casts some additional light on Hemingway's magnanimous nature. A man named Bill Lederer, who wanted to learn to write, came to Hemingway and asked for advice and guidance. Hemingway readily agreed to give him six lessons in writing in exchange for six bottles of whiskey. Lederer agreed and procured six bottles of "whiskey" at a Chinese auction. Ernest patiently presented the six lessons and duly received a bottle after each one. Lederer learned later that he had been rooked at the auction and that the bottles contained only tea. Hemingway knew this from the first, but he never mentioned it. Instead, he gave Lederer the advice, during the sessions, that he always should roll with bad luck—and never make fun of the guy who has had it. He also told Lederer that he should become highly civilized if he wished to produce meaningful writing.

On another occasion, while Martha was in Java for an extended period of time, Ernest became quite gloomy and bored. He later told a story to friends, and recounted it as an experience of Thomas Hudson in *Islands in the Stream,* about three beautiful Chinese girls with whom he had sexual experiences while Martha was gone. The girls, he said, had been a surprise gift to him from a Chinese warlord. He indicated that he had learned much from them and that the encounters had been a monumental erotic experience.

Ernest soon returned to the United States, after tedious stopovers in Manila and Guam, by way of Honolulu and San Francisco. On arriving in Key West, he was able to see his younger sons before they left to go with their mother, Pauline, to California. When she reached the West Coast, Pauline wired him that she had arrived safely. Ernest replied, indicating that he still cared for her and missed her.

In Key West, he was saddened to learn of the death of Joe Russell, who had been the owner of Sloppy Joe's Bar, and after whom Hemingway had modeled the character Harry Morgan in *To Have and Have Not*. Joe Russell had been a close friend whom Hemingway had trusted and in whom he had often confided. He would be missed.

In 1941, the Limited Editions Club announced it would award its Triennial Gold Medal to Ernest Hemingway. Sinclair Lewis was to make the presentation speech. Though Hemingway did not wish to attend, he was very eager to hear what Lewis had to say. Thus, he asked Scribner's to have a stenographer attend the event and take down what was said about him. But Scribner's failed to honor this whim. Hemingway was furious, particularly when he heard that Lewis' comments had been filled with high praise. He exploded in anger and declared that he would give the Gold Medal to Scribner's so they would never forget how inept they had been in failing to send someone to take down Lewis' comments verbatim for him to read. This is an indication of the acute and almost insatiable hunger Hemingway had for praise and acceptance from others, especially others whom he respected.

It was during this period that Hemingway attempted to improve his public image. He allowed pictures of himself to be taken that showed him to be the very genial, outdoorsy, handsome person he was. Smiling widely, he attempted to look like a movie star—and did, in fact, have a rather remarkable resemblance to Clark Gable. Hemingway was quite full of himself during these days and, buoyed by the sight of his photos in the newspapers, magazines, and newsreels, he indulged in a great deal of boasting. He seemed to be happy, self-contented, and unusually well-adjusted.

CHAPTER 10

When the Japanese bombed Pearl Harbor on December 7, 1941, Hemingway regarded it as a personal affront. He was so determined to get into the fray that he proposed to the Navy that the *Pilar* be equipped as a Q-Boat and that he be supplied with a crew and arms so he could attack the German submarines that were freely sinking Allied ships in the Caribbean. According to his strategy, if he and his crew were halted by a German submarine, they would placidly await the enemy boarding party and then suddenly open up. They would close the distance between the two ships with hidden deck-guns ablaze and even try to lob grenades into the submarine's forward hatch. Perhaps more because of who he was than for the merit of his plan, Hemingway actually convinced Naval Intelligence in Havana to equip the *Pilar* with the requested guns and a radio system. He took on a crew and gleefully started to patrol the waters, ordering his men around, inspecting the weaponry, and engaging in gunnery practice in preparation for the great sea battles that were never to occur.

In those days of 1942 in Havana, Ernest was known as a convivial, informal personality as well as a great humanist. He did not hesitate to spend money on the destitute Cubans who needed his help. In one outpouring of generosity, he bought a skiff for an impoverished Cuban fisherman. He also became known as a peacemaker, bringing together various people who were having difficulties in their relationships. Ernest was a keen observer of people and had many parties, especially on Sunday afternoons at the Finca, with the many and varied people who visited him and Martha. Throughout his life, he was deeply interested in people and in getting to know all he could about those who caught his attention. He focused so intently on whoever was talking that occasionally the person became uncomfortably aware that Ernest was staring fixedly and listening raptly to every word.

At the same time, Ernest often demonstrated a seemingly

CHAPTER 10

immature and childlike way of dealing with people. This, combined with an innately keen social perception, made him something of an enigma in many of his interpersonal relationships. One example of this behavior occurred after Martha's return to the Finca from her travels. She wanted very much to write about her experiences while they were fresh in mind. Thus, on learning that a friend's wife was en route to Cuba, she asked Ernest to meet her at the airport, for she felt the visit would consume too much of her time. Thus, on the morning of the expected arrival, Ernest drove their friend to the airport to meet his wife. He did not bother to wash or shave before going. When the friend's wife arrived, Ernest showed no affection toward her, though they all had been close in the past. The woman obviously was very hurt by this. Later, in conversation, Ernest tried to humiliate her by badgering her to agree that he had been right in "gutshooting" a dog that he thought had killed one of his cats. Cruelly, he mused that the dog had taken three days to die. His callousness reduced her to tears. But he did not stop. Instead, he went on to tell the couple that he would have shot some friends of theirs—had he known who they were—when they awakened Martha from a deep sleep by blowing a car horn beneath her window. The couple took the hint and quickly departed.

Ernest also attacked a man who formerly had been a hero of his. The assault was a verbal one and took place in the American Embassy in Cuba. Ernest belittled the man, reciting deliberate untruths about him. This incident was but another example of Ernest's often immature and unpredictable behavior.

By 1942, his relationship with Martha had become quite strained, and daily he grew more difficult to live with. His behavior could not be predicted, and often he lumbered about personally unclean and slovenly. To make matters worse, he now kept great numbers of cats around the house, and their litter added to the rank aroma. All the while, he became more egocentered, doing whatever pleased him.

The months passed, and Ernest and Martha were having "God-awful" fights. She accused him of going on submarine hunts on the *Pilar* just to obtain rationed gasoline so he and his friends could go fishing. The fury of his reaction suggests that she may have hit a bullseye. He had been drinking more and more and now had great difficulty in maintaining his emotional equilibrium. He overreacted to many situations and would strike out verbally and emotionally at the slightest provocation. Martha, according to some accounts, felt that Ernest should go to Europe, and the war, so he could become absorbed in covering the events and once more become like the man she had admired. But Ernest persisted in his activities on "patrol" in the *Pilar*.

He told many tall tales and boastful stories in those days at the Floridita Bar. When drinking, he fabricated freely and often. It was at this time that a new phenomenon, particularly intriguing to him, emerged. Many people had begun to call him "Papa." He seemed to enjoy this, since, in his view, it tended to place him on a higher level than other persons. He liked people who considered him great and were obsequious toward him in his presence.

Ernest began to project his own weaknesses onto others, especially Martha. In one such incident, he is said to have stated that men who "suffer from women" have a disease as incurable as cancer.

By the summer of 1943, Ernest and Martha were quarreling almost continually. She complained that he was so dirty she had to ask him to take a bath; but, when she did, he became infuriated. He could not dominate her as he had hoped, and he became puzzled and quite resentful when she refused to go with him, wherever and whenever he wished, on the *Pilar*. He lamented that he "suffered from women" and that they had caused him great grief. But he consoled himself with the realization that at least he had not done as Scott Fitzgerald had, and married a sick woman. In his view, a man who was truly fortunate first would be healthy—and then, if still lucky, would associate with healthy women. Ernest was quite hostile at this time and even pontificated about "trading" healthy women. He was being hurt deeply by Martha, and she, in turn, by him.

It was his pattern, at times, to develop a theme and then write a novel around it. These themes directly reflected his inner views. The cardinal message of *The Sun Also Rises* is that "Promiscuity is no solution." The point made in *To Have and Have Not* is "One man alone"—Harry Morgan's last words. In contrast, the theme of *For Whom the Bell Tolls* is "No man can be an island unto himself."

Martha finished a novel of her own and then went to England as a war correspondent for *Collier's*. Ernest missed her very much. He grew lonely and ill without her. He complained to Hadley that he was "all alone again" and had only his cats and dogs for companionship. By the end of 1943, *For Whom the Bell Tolls* had sold 785,000 copies in the United States alone. This was more than any other novel written in America during those years with the exception of *Gone With the Wind*.

In March, 1944, after her assignment in England, Martha flew to Cuba. She hoped to entice Ernest to join her in Europe to cover the war. She had arranged with a friend to get him into areas where he could cover the fighting first-hand and had talked with *Collier's* about his writing for them. As it turned out, this was only days before the Allied invasion of Europe.

CHAPTER 11

Ernest was trying intently to prove his virility in those days—both to prove it and improve it. He attempted to grow hair on his balding head by applying special solutions. On a $50 bet, he bent and broke a walking cane over his head. At parties, he often goaded people into sparring or boxing matches with him, or would have them punch him in the stomach to demonstrate the toughness of his physique.

He had accepted Martha's bid to go to Europe. When she decided to spend some time in the United States before embarking, he set out ahead of her for London. There, while waiting for Martha's ship to arrive, Ernest was involved in an auto collision. He had caught a ride home from a party with friends. Because there was a blackout, they were driving without lights. Suddenly, the car ran into a steel water tank. Ernest was seriously injured. He was rushed to a hospital, where a surgeon put 57 stitches in his knees, face and head. He also suffered a concussion and was told to not drink whiskey for some time.

To many people in London who knew him at this time, Ernest was not a likeable or attractive character. While he could be charming when he wished to be, he seemed to be playing a role, all the while appearing to be unsure what that role should be. He both hated and loved his wife, Martha, and his behavior often embarrassed her. On one occasion, he invited her to the hotel room of a friend on the pretense of taking her to dinner. When she arrived, he appeared at the door totally nude. Later that evening, Ernest went to dinner with a new acquaintance, Mary Welsh, a 36-year-old blonde from Minnesota whom he had met soon after arriving in London. She had worked as a feature writer and was the wife of an Australian reporter.

Though now suffering a constant headache resulting from his automobile accident, Hemingway became more deeply involved with Mary Welsh. He entertained her at length with sentimental accounts of his life and experiences. While he missed the *Pilar* and his friends in Cuba, and in many ways thought London strange, he also professed he liked being there.

Ernest covered much of the war in Europe from airplanes flown by the British Royal Air Force. He had some harrowing experiences while flying with the fighter pilots, to cover various aspects of the war; but, as usual, he seemingly always was testing his physical and mental endurance and courage, constantly taking risks, seeming not to care whether he was killed or not. Soon after these incidents, he wrote about them in great detail, sometimes staying up all night to record them. He had his most exciting experiences in Europe during the short time he was with one of General George Patton's armored divisions; however, he could not stand the heat and dust because of his eyes and sensitive throat. Hemingway continued to search for new adventures at the front. He wrote Mary Welsh that covering the war was for him a genuine enjoyment. He liked roughing it and proving himself over and over. He admired soldiers when they were courageous and enjoyed being in the thick of the conflict. There was something purifying about war to him, something that offered honor to all men if they proved brave and fearless.

Hemingway liked to take credit for some of the killing of the Germans and Italians by the Allied forces. He said that he hated the Germans so much that their deaths brought pleasure to him. He liked to report information about the disposition of enemy troops so that Allied commanders could take note and perhaps annihilate more of the enemy.

Martha was certainly right in believing that being at the front would invigorate Ernest and give him new life. He thoroughly enjoyed covering the war, and, during the liberation of Paris, he claimed to have personally freed several "social" institutions (such as the Travellers Club). One can picture him and his friends racing down the *Champs Elysées*, driving at top speed, and bursting through the door of the Club immediately after the last German troops had fled.

By the winter of 1944, family troubles had struck again. Martha had requested a divorce from Ernest, marking the end of his third marriage. And Ernest learned that his son, Bumby, was missing in action.

Throughout his life, Ernest had great disdain for psychologists and psychiatrists: he feared they could easily see through his makeup. He enjoyed recounting how he once had told an army divisional psychiatrist about his many cats back home in Cuba. The psychiatrist, he said, had been very accepting and had assured Ernest that there was no problem in having so many cats. With that, the author said, he told him he *did* have a problem because he wanted to have intercourse with the cats. Ernest enjoyed retelling anecdotes such as this one again and again. Since it was humorous, it put him in a positive light while putting down persons or groups he regarded with mistrust or disaffection.

Just before Christmas in 1944, Ernest had the opportunity to be with Martha in Luxembourg. He was jealous when an associate took her sleigh-riding that snowy afternoon and said he planned to take her to dinner that evening. Ernest told the man that, if he took her to dinner, *he* was going along. Soon afterward, he exasperated Martha even further when he carelessly implied that only he could get her into combat zones. Martha was incensed at his comment since she had no difficulty in getting into combat zones at will, quite on her own initiative.

One of Hemingway's troubles soon dissolved when he learned that Bumby was alive. He was in a German prisoner-of-war camp.

The news brought Hemingway great relief because he deeply loved his son. At the same time, he readily accepted his separation from Martha. He was now planning to wed Mary Welsh, as soon as her divorce was final.

But Ernest nearly destroyed his new love affair during a party and reunion with old comrades-in-arms at a local hotel. He had been given what he felt was a great gift—a pair of German machine pistols. During the party, he swaggered about with one of these, fully loaded. He seemed elated at having the pistols, having Mary, and being among old friends. At one point, he picked up a picture of Mary's first husband and set it on the mantle in front of the roomful of guests. As they looked on, he proclaimed that he would shoot it to pieces. Dissuaded from doing this, Ernest took the picture. He disappeared into the bathroom. Moments later, the guests were startled to hear two loud bursts of gunfire from the bathroom. They rushed to open the door and found that he had, indeed, shot the picture to pieces, and, in doing so, had punctured the toilet bowl, so that water was pouring over the hotel floor. Ernest thought this was highly amusing, but Mary was infuriated and reportedly nearly broke off the relationship.

CHAPTER **12**

By 1945, Ernest had returned to Cuba, where Mary was to join him later. He missed her terribly. He had never been able to live alone for long. Though he often abused people and took advantage of them, he actually needed them desperately. He longed for Mary and wrote her that he was going to read Thoreau in an effort to learn to appreciate his enforced solitude.

While Ernest waited for Mary, he complained of being beset by a general loss of memory, as well as ringing in the ears, some loss of hearing, severe headaches, and lagging speech and thought. His doctor conjectured that he had injured his health by drinking bad gin in France.

Ernest was invigorated, however, by the prospect of Mary's forthcoming arrival. He exercised regularly, played tennis, swam, sailed the *Pilar,* and seemed to be recovering mentally and physically from the rigors of covering the war.

It was good to be back in Cuba again. When Mary arrived, it marked the start of a joyous period for both of them. The tropical climate was grand, and Ernest delighted in the new things he learned about her. She was an outdoors enthusiast who loved to swim and fish. She even liked cats. To add to his happiness, Ernest learned at about this time that Bumby had been freed from the Nazi POW camp and would soon join them at the *Finca.* Ernest was proud of his son and was enormously impressed by the fact that the young man had been wounded in the right shoulder. He bragged at length to his friends about the wound and about his son's achievements in the war.

When he decided to marry Mary Welsh, Ernest sent her father a letter, which explained in detail his recent changes in religious faith and beliefs. He wrote that, when he was wounded in 1918, he was frightened of suffering and afraid he would die. Therefore, he was consumed with the desire to become a devout Catholic. He went on to say that, during the Spanish Civil War,

CHAPTER 12

he developed a disdain for the Church because of its evident alliance with the Fascists. He also described the comfort which religion brings as not without considerable cost. Then, in 1945, he said, he found he was able to get through some very rough times without praying even once. Because of his various indiscretions, he added, he felt he had given up any right to help from God in his own personal affairs, and he determined he should not pray for help no matter what befell him. He held that the Spanish Civil War changed his ideas in regard to religion, and he had now given up his faith (as did Robert Jordan in *For Whom the Bell Tolls*). With all that behind him, Ernest now felt that he was free to pursue a life of self-gratification (giving *id* a free rein, as it were).

By the end of August, 1945, Mary had left for Chicago to complete her divorce. Ernest remained in Cuba, primarily because he did not want to feel obligated to visit his aging mother, who was living in River Forest, Illinois.

While Ernest enjoyed Mary's company and missed her when she left to go to Chicago, generally, he did not like to be dependent on women. He often talked about men who had "women trouble" and about the great grief and suffering women caused. He also carped about his mother, who frequently argued with him and debated issues forcefully. In keeping with this, he was quite critical of Martha Gellhorn, his third wife, for her perverse habit of "standing her ground" against him. As the story goes, when he was leaving Pauline for Martha, he told Pauline (who had taken him from Hadley) that "those who live by the sword must die by the sword."

Significant to this is that Ernest could not tolerate weaknesses in himself or in others. One of the reasons that he disliked women so intensely was that he was dependent on them for companionship, sex, and various other creature comforts—but could not accept himself in this dependent role, which he regarded as weakness. His natural response, therefore, was to devalue the person on whom he was dependent. In fact, he did not like the idea of being dependent on *anyone,* and, as a rule, only wished women to interact with him without challenging any of his ideas or ways. Little did he realize that this was a symptom of his human weakness—the characteristic of which he was so intolerant when seeing it in others.

During this period in 1945, Hemingway was having difficulty getting back to writing. There were various visitors to his home who consumed much of his time, but his real problem was just getting back to the discipline and the routine of writing. He had been involved in a great many exciting adventures while covering the war in Europe. Now, writing about them seemed a bore—a poor substitute for the exploits themselves. Yet, he was eager to get back to being productive in order to increase his feelings of adequacy.

At this time, Hemingway wrote a manifesto declaring that men had a responsibility, during peacetime, to debate issues, to protest, and to rebel. He felt that, during periods of war, men needed to understand the importance of courage, obedience, and discipline; but, in peacetime, they should work out their differences in honest, if at times heated, debate. These are principles which he felt should be followed by nations and peoples of the world. Yet, ironically, in his personal life, he could tolerate little debate or disagreement with any of his views.

By 1946, Ernest was working on a new novel called *The Garden of Eden*. He revealed to friends that he had never been able to outline a book before writing it and then stick to the outline. Instead, he conjured events as he went along, seldom knowing what was going to happen next in any given manuscript. In *The Garden of Eden*, Ernest wrote of private games in which his characters, David and Catherine, exchanged roles, even to their names, in their sex play. Another couple portrayed in the work spent months exploring ways whereby they could come to resemble each other physically—a curious and revealing turn of Ernest's mind. That he intellectually antedated the unisex phenomenon in world culture by nearly a quarter of a century perhaps speaks less of prescience than of hidden longings. Brandishing the macho masculine superstructure about requires so much mental energy that some creative males might well entertain the fantasy of what life would be like to relax the façade—in the privacy of an intimate relationship or in safely projecting these impulses onto characters in a tale.

CHAPTER 13

Ernest Hemingway and Mary Welsh were "married" twice—the first ceremony being most informal (as neither was legally free to marry), romantic, and charming.

It consisted of beautiful and selfless thoughts, articulated at the Ritz in Paris late in 1944. The lovers declared that they would cleave together following their own rules of conduct—living, loving, making gifted children, and writing in an aura of respect for one another's talents and needs. Worthy of the rationalizations of Henry VIII (but free from his annoying, even mystifying superego), this idyllic arrangement augured to provide a climate in which greater literature could evolve for the benefit of mankind.

Their legal marriage, performed by a rather drably uninspiring drone of a civil functionary of Cuban origin, took place in a dingy office in Havana on March 14, 1946. The ceremony consumed the day, in two tiring segments fraught with unforeseen complications of inane proportions. The day ended, at the *Finca*, in a verbal battle which Ernest sorely needed to ventilate his frustration over the anticlimactic experience. It very nearly was disastrous, as Mary packed and might have chucked the marriage on the spot, except that fatigue prevented it.

In July of 1947, Mary learned that she was pregnant, and she and Ernest made plans to go to Sun Valley, Idaho. Ernest looked forward to substantial hunting trips and had accumulated 10,000 shotgun cartridges, as well as 2,000 rounds of rifle ammunition.

The many sides of Ernest Hemingway constantly surprised even those who were closest to him. A good example of this occurred while he and Mary were in Casper, Wyoming, on the way to Idaho. While Ernest was outside of the motel, preparing the car for the day's trip, Mary began to have horrible pains. Her pregnancy was ectopic, and the left fallopian tube had ruptured. Ernest rushed her to the local hospital. There, he learned the surgeon was away, and Mary, attended by an intern, hovered near death all day. Finally, her veins collapsed, and she lost consciousness. The intern told Ernest that his wife was going to die. Undaunted, Ernest put on a surgeon's gown and had the intern probe for a vein in which to inject life-saving plasma. He then assisted in various ways and stayed with her until her respiration was normal and the surgeon had returned. Mary spent a week inside an oxygen tent. She knew that she had almost died; she never forgot what Ernest had done. He, in turn, was deeply impressed by her bravery and fascinated to discover that, as he described it, "Fate could be fucked."

Ernest continued to overdo his valuing of courage. On one occasion, in 1947, he exploded in anger on learning that William Faulkner had said he lacked the courage to experiment in his writing as others, such as Dos Passos, Caldwell, and Wolfe, had done. Ernest immediately enlisted a friend to write Faulkner and give him a detailed account of Ernest's activities at the front during the war. Faulkner later wrote him a letter of apology.

In October, 1948, Ernest became quite fearful for his health: he had begun to hear strange, humming sounds in his head. At this time, he was seriously overweight, at 256 pounds, and his physician was quite concerned about his high blood pressure, which had reached 215/125.

By July of the following year, Ernest had lost some of the weight, had his hypertension under better control, and he and Mary were again in Cuba. He celebrated his birthday that year with an all-day fishing trip. He took along Mary and some close friends, who had brought aboard many presents for him. They enjoyed champagne and caviar, and a wonderful time was had by all.

In the months that followed, Ernest made additional trips to Europe. He was enamored of Venice and particularly impressed by a girl named Adriana whom he had met there. When he returned to Cuba, he resumed seeing his old friends and attempted to hunt and fish. He was feeling somewhat frustrated and distressed, however, especially in regard to Adriana, who kept intruding into his thoughts. He explained his depression to others, however, by attributing it to boredom, having too much pride, and having to distrust so many people. Once again, he began talking of suicide.

It was in 1950 that *Across The River and into the Trees* was published. The reviews of the book were bad, to say the least. Critics called it "distressing and embarrassing" and said that Hemingway had shrunk in stature as an author.

Adriana arrived in Cuba on October 28, 1950, chaperoned by her mother. Ernest and Mary met them and helped them through

Immigration. They stayed with the Hemingways and had a most enjoyable time. Ernest again was invigorated and renewed by a woman's presence. Adriana was a young and pretty girl, and she seemed to help him regain his resolve to write. By February, 1951, he had finished the book on which he was working: *The Old Man and the Sea*.

That same year, he approached the completion of another book, which would be titled *Islands in the Stream*. The central character of the work is Thomas Hudson. The story deals with the search for a crew of a sunken German submarine in the Caribbean. It was based on an actual experience Ernest had on the *Pilar* during World War II when he and his crew had recklessly pursued a submarine.

In 1951, Ernest's mother died. At this same time, Mary's father grew very ill with cancer. Ernest became more and more aware of death because of these sad events and began to give his own mortality a great deal of morbid thought. He believed that death comes in multiples to significant people. This idea was soon reinforced when Pauline, his second wife, died in California. Pauline was fifty-six years of age and had died of a tumor of the adrenal medulla. Ernest, overwhelmed by her death, reflected on his life with her. He once had loved her dearly and later had rejected her.

Ernest turned again to his writing. While in Cuba, he was able to work very well. He really seemed to have gotten back into writing. He also wrote many warm, friendly letters to various acquaintances, such as Marlene Deitrich, of whom he was very fond. At this time, *The Old Man and the Sea* was published in *Life Magazine* as well as in book form, which pleased him greatly. The work was to bring him a Pulitzer Prize and the Nobel Prize for literature. As with all awards and other forms of positive recognition, these tributes delighted him and sent his spirits soaring.

Soon after these events, Ernest and Mary went to Europe. They spent some time in Spain and then went on to British East Africa, where he devoted himself to leopard and lion hunting. While in Africa, the Hemingways chartered a four-place Cessna single-engine aircraft from which they planned to see Victoria Falls. While in flight, they suddenly encountered a flock of ibis. They tried to maneuver away from the birds, only to strike a telephone line, the impact of which caused them to crash. Mary was the more seriously injured, with two cracked ribs. Ernest set up shelter. They were on the ground all that night with little sleep or rest owing to the wild animals, which were constantly skulking about their frail shelter. At last, they were able to catch a ride on a launch up-river to a local village. There, they rented another plane. On takeoff, however, the plane promptly crashed and burned. Ernest was badly hurt. His spine was injured, and he was reported bleeding from "every orifice of his body." The impact also had caused the displacement of some of his internal organs. This, plus the shock of the second crash, was horrendous to both of them.

By this time, the wreckage of the first plane had been spotted and word had gone out to the world that the Hemingways had perished. In the days that followed, Ernest had the macabre experience of reading his own obituaries in various newspapers from throughout the world.

Ernest recuperated slowly from his injuries. He returned to his writing, buoyed by reports that his book *The Old Man and the Sea* was selling well. It would soon be made into a motion-picture.

In the fall of 1955, Ernest worked on film sequences of *The Old Man and the Sea* with Spencer Tracy and found this activity new and challenging.

During this time, the Castro guerilla movement was spreading across eastern Cuba. Life in Havana and its environs was becoming more and more fearful and anxiety-ridden for everyone. On one occasion, the Batista troops entered the *Finca* and searched it for arms. At the appearance of the strangers, Ernest's favorite dog, "Black Dog," growled and barked loudly, defending their home. He was struck with a rifle butt and killed. Ernest was incensed. He went immediately to the government offices to register a vociferous protest. This action won him great respect from the intimidated Cuban people, and word of it spread rapidly.

The political conditions in Cuba grew more unfavorable daily. Ernest decided it might be wise to move to Idaho. He was having considerable problems with depression at this time and began to manifest obvious difficulties in answering questions. He had lost a lot of weight and had lost confidence, as well, in his ability to express himself verbally.

In November, 1960, Hemingway entered the Mayo Clinic under a fictitious name. His blood pressure was 220/125. He was diagnosed as having a mild form of diabetes mellitus, the same disease that had precipitated his father's suicide. Test results also indicated that he might have hemochromatosis, a rare disease with a most dismal prognosis. His blood pressure soon subsided to 138/80, and he felt better. But, by March, he was again in the grip of depression.

Later, Hemingway readmitted himself to the Mayo Clinic, this time under his own name. He underwent electroshock treatments, which seemed to help alleviate the depression. However, they also affected his recall. In this, the shock treatments had a circularly negative effect. While somewhat relieved of his depression, Hemingway also became unable to remember events. This was deeply distressing to him since it interfered with his craft, which was contingent upon what was stored in the cerebral neurons now stoned into muteness by the cataclysmic electrical shocks. Thus, the circularity had an an ironic outcome. His memories of grander times, forever lost, had led to depression; this prompted him to undergo shock therapy, which convulses and sweeps away recollections wherein genius lies entrapped; his memories gone, he experienced despair at the loss of something he could only sense; and this led him to depression again, but now experienced in its ultimate form—futility. This futility, together with delusions and despair, surrounded Hemingway just before his death.

On his final day, July 2, 1961, Ernest Hemingway selected the same method that he had described years before to others as a respectable blueprint for suicide. He placed a shotgun against his head and depressed the trigger with his toe. The man who lived to write, to hunt, and to make love, was dead. His temporal stay on Earth had spanned 62 years.

His suicide was both predictable and preventable by competents within a class he scorned, possibly through fear. Psychological or psychiatric intervention, enlisted and employed, may have kept this mind and spirit with us a while. The electroshocked brain cells gradually would have yielded up their locked-in core, and who can speculate what other powerful constructs his literary legacy might have included?

In destroying himself, Ernest Hemingway killed something in us. Intellectual appetite is such that a rigorously developed craft and form generates a desire, even a demand for more of its fruits. And true creative genius may have imitators—but we mourn the loss of a master from our midst.

PSYCHOLOGICAL EVALUATION
ERNEST HEMINGWAY

General Physical and Psychological Characteristics

Ernest Hemingway was born on July 21, 1899. He died on July 2, 1961 as a result of a self-inflicted gunshot wound. Physical characteristics: he was six feet tall and normally weighed about 210 pounds; however, he tended to be overweight, and at one time reached a weight of 260 pounds. He had brown eyes, a ruddy complexion, very large feet, and, in his younger years, thick, straight, brownish-black hair. Later, during his fifties, he was balding, with thin, sparse white hair. His beard, black in his youth, later turned brown, and then, totally white.

He favored casual clothing and open-necked shirts, not wanting to feel confined. He had a slight speech impediment which caused the letters "i" and "r" to take on the sound of "w".

Physical Ailments During His Lifetime

Hemingway was born healthy. However, he had imperfect vision; from birth, his left eye was weaker than his right. In 1918, he was wounded, taking more than 200 pieces of shrapnel in his legs. In 1927, a cut foot became infected with anthrax, which resulted in 10 days in bed with severe swelling and fever. He developed severe liver problems in 1938, for which he was medicated; he also received typhoid shots. In 1941, severe sunburn resulted in his nose peeling and his ankles swelling. Reportedly, this was the beginning of the skin cancer condition that was to plague him for the rest of his life. An auto accident in 1944 resulted in wounds that required 57 stitches and caused him to have headaches for several months. That same year, while covering the war in Europe, he also demonstrated an intolerance to heat, dust and noise. In 1947, he began to experience a humming sound in his head; his blood pressure was found to be 215/125, and his weight had increased to 256 pounds. In 1949, he was confined to bed for two weeks with severe chest colds. Thereafter, he experienced problems with his left eye that led to a highly contagious infection, believed to have resulted from dust particles. The infection spread across his face. Penicillin was prescribed to check the infection.

In 1950, another skin infection developed. The diagnosis indicated Hemingway was allergic to gunpowder. Penicillin again was prescribed, along with aureomycin and ichthyol ointment. That same year, severe pains developed in his right leg. X-rays indicated the presence of several fragments of encysted metal, pieces of the shrapnel imbedded since his wartime injuries in 1918.

The hypertension condition which had manifested in 1947 reoccurred in 1960. In this same year, he also learned that he had a mild case of diabetes mellitus. His weight now was down to 175 pounds. Tests disclosed he had an enlarged liver resulting from heavy and extended use of alcohol and possibly also due to a rare disease called hemochromatosis. He declined to have a biopsy that would clarify whether or not he had the disease. His blood pressure during this period ranged up to 220/150 owing to acute anxiety. Further drug treatment seemed to result in depression, so he was advised against taking drugs for a time. Electroshock treatments were prescribed at the rate of two a week during December, 1960 and January, 1961 to help alleviate his depression. However, his despair deepened, due to his loss of recall. The shock treatments were continued in order to counteract the debilitating melancholia and the delusions he was experiencing. During this period, his weight increased to 260 pounds, considerably higher than his normal weight of 210.

In this final period of his life, Hemingway was troubled by insomnia most of the time and, for long periods, was unable to establish wholesome and restful sleep patterns.

Specific Psychological Characteristics

Throughout most of his life, Hemingway had a great yearning, almost a lust, for the knowledge and fullness of life. He sought out life in both the world's brightest and darkest regions. He was pragmatic, yet, at times, rigidly moralistic—an ambivalence that caused him severe grief in his quest to experience life at its fullest. This can be noted in the guilt feelings that resulted from activities he regarded as immoral (for example, his leaving his first wife for another woman). He was overwhelmed by the constant feeling that life is forever fraught with pain. He told himself and his friends that he was never frightened, but the psychological nuances of his life and work seem to point up that, in fact, he was a man who feared life itself and what might come after. Overcompensation was a common characteristic of his behavior, which is merely one example of this compensatory mechanism in operation.

Hemingway was highly competitive and ambitious. He did not take failure well and characteristically exaggerated or lied about his shortcomings. His personal search for identity is revealed in the ways he manipulated the major characters in his writings, having them play out various roles in scenarios into which he could project his own restless nature. He would propel these characters into different types of problematic situations, as though to see how he himself might react in such circumstances. Most novelists, of course, indulge in this vicarious activity.

It is our belief that Hemingway had strong feelings of inadequacy with regard to his sexual prowess and that many of the sexual affairs he recounted were fabrications or exaggerations dropped on friends for effect. We also believe that he may have been impotent during periods of his life and may well have suffered a great deal of psychosexual confusion. This we surmise from writings about him, and by him, revealing his seemingly strong negative feelings toward dependence upon women and his inability to tolerate their competitiveness. One of his great fears in life was inadequacy, and some statements about women in his books as well as to his friends tend to raise serious questions about his own view of his masculine identity.

In dealing with his ideas concerning his sexuality and the psychosexual confusion, which psychologists might conclude surfaced, at least in his mind, during his thirties and forties, Hemingway appears to have overreacted to and overcompensated for fears of sexual inadequacy. It is curious that, although Hemingway examines innumerable problems of the human condition in his books, the subject of homosexuality or bisexuality is never treated in any definitive manner by so keen and perceptive a writer.

One might wonder if, psychologically, Hemingway was not somewhat naive, possibly not understanding that most persons experience some homosexual feelings during their lives. Many men never recover from this experience, which often occurs as an exploratory encounter during boyhood, and go through life always secretly questioning their heterosexuality and their sexual adequacy. While we have no evidence that Hemingway thought much about homosexuality, we do feel he was often preoccupied with concerns about sexual inadequacy. Evidence seems to indicate that these questions came to the fore in his thirties and forties, when he was eager to experience every aspect of himself and constantly was exploring his own tendencies as well as those of others.

Women who threatened him intellectually, or in other manifestations of their assertiveness, certainly were not his favorites. However, while being a very physical man, he admired women who could bring him information that was of value to him in his own professional growth and development. Conversely, he demonstrated little attraction to overly dependent females who required a great deal from him, especially his time and his having to do "nice things" for them.

Hemingway's great talent was that he was a brilliant social observer, and, in this observation, he never flagged. We feel that intelligence testing, had he undergone such tests during his thirties, would have indicated he was of superior intellect. He had a high social intelligence, which was of great help to him in observing and understanding people; however, he did not always use this social intelligence to facilitate his personal interactions with others. The main reason for this may have been his interest in experiencing others, pushing them to their limits to see how they would respond, often losing friends by expecting too much of them. He required adulation, and people who did not constantly reinforce his need to be admired soon lost his favor. He seemed hypocritical in many ways, often surrounding himself with people whom he really did not like in order to use them for their experiences and what they could add to his experiential base, and thus, to his books.

Hemingway was constantly searching for meaning and truth and had a great deal of trouble finding both. Periodically, he scoffed at religion and, at times, even carried "lucky stones." He was somewhat superstitious and for years wore a leather vest to protect his kidneys from viral influences.

He could be proper, as well as gracious and warmly affectionate with friends. He also seemed to need to pigeonhole people either as "good guys" or "bad guys." This reflects a basic inability to deal with ambiguity and is in conflict with his keen ability for social observation. Hemingway had difficulty with the concept that "good guys" could be rotters, on occasion, and that "bad guys" could sometimes prove out good—a handicapping form of tunnel-vision even in an artist of lesser stature.

He was quite temperamental, and, in terms of psychiatric categories, he occasionally demonstrated strong manic-depressive characteristics. He spoke of suicide throughout his life and was plagued with physical and hypochondriacal problems. However, when actually sick, he enjoyed overcoming whatever illness dared intrude into his life space. He enjoyed testing himself but disliked being tested by others, especially in verbal competition; this was particularly insufferable when his opponent was an aggressive, verbally capable and bright female. By addressing pretty women as "daughter," he immediately ranked them beneath himself and allowed a degree of self-aggrandizement, which, in his estimation, cast him either as the wise father or the strong, protective big brother.

Hemingway's psychological characteristics become even more apparent when observed in terms of transactional analysis. The language of transactional analysis has been popularized in recent years by the books, *I'm OK, You're OK* by Dr. Thomas Harris and *Games People Play* by the late Dr. Eric Berne. The following is a brief description of the terms and principles which are useful in understanding transactional analysis.

Structural Analysis: The interrelationship of three discrete parts—Parent (P), Adult (A), and Child, (C)—of the individual personality.

Transactional Analysis: The interrelationship of the PAC of one person with that of another.

Parent: The ego state that incorporates the feelings, behavior and attitudes of one's parents. Behavior generally is either judgmental (demanding, critical) or nurturing. Such behavior is displayed by an individual acting from this state.

Adult: The ego state that gathers data from the other internal ego states and the external world, subjects it to reality testing, probability estimation, and logical computation, and then chooses the most appropriate course of behavior.

Child: The ego state that is intuitive, creative, feeling, sensuous, and loving. This state can be one of total self-centeredness or one of adaptability, in terms of either giving in or obeying the commands of the parental figure.

Script: The basic position from which the individual is acting out his life, using the data that he has gathered during his childhood through both cognition and feeling. The individual decides whether he is essentially lovable or unlovable, and positions himself on a continuum of lovability versus unlovability.

Hemingway most often dealt with people in two ways. One way was as child to adult. In this position, he tested limits and took the child's role, almost asking others to dictate his next logical course of action. He did this in particular through his "I want what I want when I want it" approach. This child-like behavior was seen during periods when he was frustrated by not reaching some of his goals, as well as after he had reached many of his immediate goals but found them short of his expectations. He was heavily self-centered, demanding and often defiant toward others who were attempting to be friendly or to achieve closeness with him.

The other Hemingway approach was that of the parent to child. In this position, he often took on the behavior of a parental figure and was quite judgmental, demanding and critical in his relationships with others. A prime example of this is his referring to women as "daughter" thus elevating himself to a type of nurturing fatherly role.

The key point to be made in this transactional analysis look at Hemingway is that he seldom dealt with other individuals as adults. In other words, he did not offer himself as an adult figure, taking responsibility, making logical decisions, and discussing issues with other individuals while allowing them to play adult roles. The fact that he so often positioned himself in either a child-parent or parent-child mode in his relationships with others reflects his constant effort to deal with his feelings of inadequacy.

Each of his four wives, in turn, found the best way to keep Hemingway at the task of writing was to assume the role of parent to his willful child: he had to feel their constant reinforcement, their nurturing and sustenance, in order to stay on his creative course. Remarkably, they found subsequent opportunity to form friendships with one another in a unique manner, almost like an extended family unit.

Ernest's relationship with his parents was not a happy one. He was always envious of and competitive with his father, and, in later years, described his hatred of his mother as non-Freudian, saying that she was an "all-American bitch." He felt that his father was cowardly, and he disliked any show of weakness on the part of the human male. Since he could not compete with his father academically, and, in his early years, he could not compete physically, he attempted to discredit him. He wanted deeply to have the love of his mother, and when both she and Dr. Hemingway classified their son's literary work as "immoral portrayals," Ernest was deeply wounded.

Ernest was like most men in that he sought to achieve balance or equilibrium in the basic drives of his life. He often was off-balance because he felt he needed to conceal all of his physical weaknesses; but, in attempting to cover them up by various types of endurance tests, he actually called the attention of the world to them. The result was that any inadequacies on his part, especially those related to physical capabilities, were emphasized, and Ernest's inability to accept any shortcoming was aggravated even more. His constant discussions in his writings of his characters' physical abilities drew to him, through identification, the critical words of many whom he admired and others he came to hate, especially literary critics.

At the same time, Hemingway was keenly aware that stress

is a necessary ingredient for growth and development; he put himself in various stressful situations to test his abilities and see in what direction he might grow. Hemingway had great trouble coping with periods of quiet and non-involvement. He needed excitement and high levels of emotional participation in order to be happy. He destroyed relationships with friends, wives, and others, only to attempt later to rebuild them, learn from what happened, and use the information in one way or another. He was capable of great cruelty to those he disliked, including his former friends. He often came across more as a taker and a user than as a giver. He also was a person of considerable wit who enjoyed quick, verbal footwork, especially in the presence of women whom he wished to impress.

Ernest firmly believed that great creativity could come only when one was deeply in love, and he loved frequently—too frequently, in fact, to maintain his equilibrium in terms of society's requirements. After his fourth marriage, he felt as much pressured to be married as after his first or second. One of his problems was that he never was able simply to live with a woman without taking the final marital step. He needed to be in accord with his religion and needed the approval of his fellow man. However, his search for meaning through constant complex relationships included the destruction of relationships with significant women and the beginning of new ones.

Frequently, Ernest felt overburdened with stress. Because he was constantly seeking growth and development, he often involved himself in stress-laden situations. When a person is coping with existing stresses, he is highly intolerant to unforeseen additional stress, and Ernest was no exception. This accounts in part for his mood vacillations: he could change almost immediately from being warmly affable to being totally obnoxious with the same group.

Hemingway lived in a time when many of the societal and cultural anchor points that had given emotional security to millions over the years were starting to be substantially threatened. Man was becoming depersonalized in the growth of mass culture. The breakdown of traditional religious faiths gave rise to growing confusion about the meaning of the human condition. Hemingway was one of those who felt alienated and estranged. He was constantly looking for his god and trying to conceptualize what God really meant to him. He was making a constant effort to verify his existence by trying to understand other men. He searched for meaning in his life by keenly observing others. He was plagued by feelings of anxiety and guilt, resulting from his great need to realize his potentialities. Spurred by this drive to achieve, he brought great despair to his family, other loved ones and friends. This is reflected in part by his several marriages and his use and characterization of his friends in his novels, as often occurred, to their bewilderment and personal hurt.

He made great efforts at self-definition, and when he found a concept that had meaning for him, he grasped it so tightly that the meaning often became distorted. The best example of this was his great love of hunting, which he carried to such an extreme that on, occasions, he slaughtered literally hundreds of game birds.

Hemingway experienced considerable conflict in his search for the meaning of life. All rational human beings have a common characteristic that can be defined as a will to meaning. This is the search for satisfying values, and it is a highly individual matter. Ernest wanted almost desperately to believe in the Church and its teachings, but he used it just as he used people—for his own aims and his own objectives. When he was seriously wounded in the Spanish Civil War, he relied heavily on religious faith to pull him through; however, when later he wished to divorce Hadley, he claimed that she had not been a member of the Church and, therefore, his marriage was not "of" the Church and could be ended without offending that institution.

While Ernest maneuvered and manipulated in his goal-oriented manner, he was unable to escape the accompanying destruction of some of his beliefs about moral standards which he had carried over from his early training. This inevitably gave rise to considerable conflict and despair, which were to compound as his life went on. His selective use of the Church to suit his whims or purposes at a given time created a discordance with his underlying value system that may have inspired the writing of his famous "Nada" stanzas, which, in effect, indicate that there is nothing and will be nothing, and that all is for naught. We feel this early writing reflects the emptiness he felt at times and is a portent of the depth into which his despair ultimately would plunge him.

From a psychological point of view, Ernest had far more opportunity to self-actualize, or to become a fully functioning person, than most persons ever have. In other words, he had the license and opportunity to be his "own man." In later years, he was not forced to do any work other than writing for a living and thus was free to explore his own thinking and the thinking of others. He also was free to search out life experiences that held promise for building his psychological maturation and for bringing him fulfillment and self-actualization. He then took on, in effect, the responsibility for evaluating his own progress toward becoming an optimal person in terms of his own goal structure. When he reached many of his goals as a novelist, he became dissatisfied with himself. It was said by some of his disillusioned associates that his idiosyncratic, boorish behavior was far greater than should be tolerated in the name of creativity. That is, those who knew him best felt that his obnoxious behavior, almost antisocial on occasions, was not justified by the level of his creative genius. Hemingway became aware of this opinion on the part of some, and a vicious circle developed. He needed the approval of others, wanted it badly, and yet was so egocentric that he felt he should be loved and admired no matter how he treated people. In his later life, this caused him even greater guilt, anxiety, and despair, yet he was not willing to abandon what he felt was his "right" to treat people just as he wished. Our feeling is that he believed that some of his critical and abusive conduct toward others was unnecessary and unauthentic. In other words, he recognized that some of his behavior might well have been for the purposes of exhibition and "attention-getting."

Hemingway was most happy when he was deeply involved in his writing. He had a somewhat "manic-depressive" or cyclothymic approach to his work, characterized by prolonged periods of hyperactivity or overactivity, punctuated by moods of depression and underactivity. When he was writing, he was less active sexually, according to his own accounts, due to his being almost totally engrossed in his writing and subject matter. When he was underactive or underproductive in his writing, he was depressed. To combat this depression, he attempted to write during some barren periods when he really had nothing to say. Recognizing this led him to actively seek out more new physical and mental challenges to relieve his fear that his creativity was drying up.

It should be noted that periods of cyclical mood elevation and depression which have been associated with manic-depressive reactions usually are interspersed with periods of relative normalcy. Without saying that, in later years, Ernest Hemingway was a manic-depressive psychotic, we feel his documented behavior is consistent with manic-depressive tendencies that later yielded a fixed depression from which he could not recover.

There are many theories used to explain and predict (and thus, sometimes head off) suicide. One theory which has substantial support is what might be called the "cybernetic" view. This theory holds that the brain functions in a logical, rational manner. It evaluates situations, determines the alternatives of action, attaches probability estimations to these alternatives, and then directs the individual to adopt the course of action which has the highest probability of being effective. Most, and sometimes all, of this decision-making process is totally unconscious; that is, at best, the person may be only dimly aware of this thought process.

In the case of suicide, the individual's behavior is completely logical from his vantage point and from his evaluation of the facts at hand. While one may feel that Ernest Hemingway's decision to commit suicide was illogical, the accomplishment is a haunting reality. We feel that Hemingway considered many factors, most of which are unknown to us. These included his dwindling vitality, proliferating health problems, increasing age, declining ability to write creatively, diminishing virility, and so forth. Confronted with this set of facts, and probably others more obscure, he explored and evaluated various alternatives for action. His search obviously turned up no viable options. The most acceptable manner in which he could proceed, in his view, was to terminate his existence.

Many psychologists feel suicide can be predicted, the key predictive factor lying in the individual's view of death. If a person looks at death as one of the viable solutions available in problematical situations, the probability of suicide is greatly increased. Ernest Hemingway, from his statements and his writings, viewed death as an option and a readily available means of escaping from the problems of contemporary reality. He ruminated about his own suicide while still in his early twenties. Perhaps even more significant, he saw death as a solution or natural ending for the dilemmas of many of the significant characters in his writings. There is an impressively long list of characters who die, or seem to, in Hemingway's stories. Many of these figures seemingly were gratuitously written into oblivion by Hemingway, though this likely was the author symptomatically turning his own aggressive drives back upon himself. In real life, Ernest's father committed suicide—as did Hadley's.

When Hemingway, by his own evaluation, felt he had lost his ability to write, he said that he had trouble making love, was unable to hunt, and admitted an increasing feeling of despair. He was having difficulty in dealing with the fact that he was growing older; however, in our opinion, the main depressive aspect of his later life was that he was unable to keep his life moving on a plane of high excitement, exploiting the energy and activity that had been so reliable in his adventurous earlier years. He grew discouraged, and his zest for life waned. Writing became a very difficult, almost impossible task. He sought treatment for depression through electroshock treatment, but one side effect was forgetfulness, which caused him even more depression because the memories that provided the ideas for his writing no longer welled up readily. Hemingway became increasingly plagued by feelings of unworthiness, dominated by distress at the shock-induced sluggishness of his thought processes. He pondered about suicide, and his family and friends feared that it might become a reality.

When an individual is having a depressive reaction, he usually feels that his ailments and difficulties are his due as punishment for various mistakes and sins he has committed. Since Ernest had been plagued with guilt feelings throughout his life, especially since his divorce from Hadley (from which he never fully recovered), he attributed his depression to real as well as imagined reasons. When these factors were superimposed on his physical condition, which consisted, at the time, of hypertension, encroaching diabetes mellitus, possible hemochromatosis, and the memory deficits resulting from electroshock treatments, the idea of suicide as a viable escape method grew irresistible.

Hemingway had been obsessed with the concept of suicide throughout his life. It is ironic that the shotgun blast which killed him could be considered a last, all-out effort for attention, again overplayed. Before committing this final act, he may well have recalled the time when the world had paid so much attention to him after his "death" had been announced (wrongly, of course) as a result of the plane crash in Africa. Eagerly, and with great amusement, he had read the newspaper accounts of his reported demise, and he talked about the plane crash with high enthusiasm on several occasions shortly before the actuality of his death.

Hemingway's depression, characterized by a predominant mood of futility associated with his inability to live life to the fullest—when combined with his love of the heights of emotional experience now forever past and perhaps even some curiosity about the adventure of suicide and death—led inexorably to the final act—self-destruction.

In gestalt psychology, the concept is offered that the whole is greater than the sum of its parts. Hemingway was ingenious in breaking the whole into many parts and manipulating them in a complex style to create the mental pictures for which his writings have become world-famous. A childhood devotee of Mark Twain, whom he came to idolize, Hemingway spent a lifetime developing his craft to the point where it could rival Twain's in clarity—a feat which enabled him to appeal to all levels of literary taste and comprehension. His works were read and discussed from around pot-bellied stoves in rural America to the highest halls of learning both here and throughout the world. He wrote about events, people, and things in a lucid fashion, pulling no punches. Thus, he was able to succeed, with limited psychological insight into the motivations of his characters, by virtue of the richness of his language and style. Heidegger has said that "thinking must learn again to descend into the poverty of its materials." Hemingway disliked abstractions and essentially scorned philosophical concepts. He chose instead to reduce abstractions to their elemental and purely descriptive terms as his way of illuminating the lives of his characters, embroiled, for the most part, in violent contests for survival.

In his own contest against the forces of darkness, Hemingway is reflected as a hearty and physical man constantly testing his strength and courage in an endeavor to experience every aspect of life to its fullest. A complex personality, he radiated an aura that commanded attention throughout a dramatic, full and productive life. But the stresses of physical infirmities, aging, and fear that his creativity had abandoned him—as his courage never had—took their toll. And, death had claimed so many of his friends.

Thirteen years before his death, Hemingway wrote a melancholy but revealing letter about significant people who had been important to him who were no longer alive. He described them as "the great deads," thus suggesting a concept not alien to readers of Kurt Vonnegut, Jr.—that death is merely a temporal event, not necessarily an ending.

Hemingway's letter, written in 1948, seems to convey his feeling that death is simply another dimension that has no bearing on unique personality patterns. Another way of explaining this is that "the deads" do not enter a collective state wherein they all become anonymous. A dead Gertrude Stein is *still that individual* (who also happens to be dead from a physical point of view). Fitzgerald? He is still as he was when Hemingway knew him. Picasso remains an artist. They are not like the other deads, any more than they were like them in this life.

On July 2, 1961, seeing more on the other side than he felt he had here, Hemingway opted to hurl himself into another quest for high adventure.

We can only wish him well.